the
Undertaker's
wife

the Undertaker's *wife*

WISDOM AND MUSINGS;
Life in a Small Town Funeral Home.

CELIA M. HASTINGS

foreword by David Buttrick and Helen DeVos

FaithWalk
PUBLISHING
Grand Haven, Michigan

©2005 Celia M. Hastings
Published by FaithWalk Publishing
Grand Haven, Michigan 49417

Scripture quotations, unless otherwise indicated, are taken from the HOLY BIBLE, NEW INTERNATIONAL VERSION®. NIV®. Copyright ©1973, 1978, 1984 by International Bible Society. Used by permission of Zondervan. All rights reserved.

Scripture quotations marked KJV are taken from the Holy Bible, King James Version, Cambridge, 1769.

Scripture quotations marked NRSV are taken from The Holy Bible: New Revised Standard Version/Division of Christian Education of the National Council of Churches of Christ in the United States of America. Nashville: Thomas Nelson Publishers, ©1989. Used by permission. All rights reserved.

Printed in the United States of America
10 09 08 07 06 05   7 6 5 4 3 2 1

Library of Congress Cataloging-in-Publication Data

Hastings, Celia M.
  The undertaker's wife : wisdom and musings : life in a small town funeral home / by Celia M. Hastings.—1st ed.
      p. cm.
  Includes bibliographical references.
  ISBN-10: 1-932902-51-1 (pbk. : alk. paper)
  ISBN-13: 978-1-932902-51-8
  1. Death—Social aspects. 2. Bereavement. 3. Grief. 4. Funeral rites and ceremonies. 5. Burial. I. Title.
  HQ1073.H38 2005
  306.9'0973—dc22
                          2005008385

Dedication

In loving memory of
Grant and Opal

With love to
John, Paul
and Joy

In eager expectation of
Grant Joseph

Contents

Foreword

There are few books about a small-town funeral home. Even fewer are about the wife of a funeral director. And virtually none are about an undertaker's wife with an advanced theological degree. Here you hold in your hands *The Undertaker's Wife,* by the remarkable Celia Hastings, an absolutely unique book by a fine writer with a friendly voice.

Some years ago, after the World Trade Center Towers tumbled and the U.S. was tooling up for retribution, I was running errands in a small northern Michigan village. At Susie's restaurant, I spotted a stack of purple construction paper. I picked up a sheet and discovered that someone had printed a few biblical texts:

> *Love your enemies … Pray for them.*
> *Do not return evil for evil.*
> *Overcome evil with good.*

As I took care of errands, I discovered similar stacks of paper—in the farm co-op, the photography store, the party store—all over the village. I wondered, *Was there a stack at the Gold Nugget Bar as well?* Someone in town was bold enough to question our American military eagerness for retribution and to do so on the basis of early Christian teachings (Romans 12:14–21). Normally, in the midst of military excursions the nonviolent words of Christian Scripture are lost in the din of patriotic hoopla—particularly in small-town America where village parks often sport memorial weaponry from World War II. So someone in the village was not afraid to be an independent thinker! After a while, I asked around and finally ended up writing my letter to a "Ms. Celia Hastings":

November 18, 2001

Dear Ms. Hastings:

This past September after the Trade Towers tumbled into dust I was in [the village] and picked up one of the purple "hand-outs" you prepared. The quotations you printed on the sheets of paper, drawing from Sermon on the Mount texts and Romans 12, were apt and splendid.

Last week I was lecturing at the Washington, D.C., National Cathedral, and I told my audience about the pages you placed all over the village. So, guess what? You reached the village, but also an audience in Washington, D.C. And, oddly enough, I was delivering what was called "The Hastings Lecture."

I wanted to thank you for your courage and your faith.

The next summer I was able to meet Celia Hastings face to face; she and her multitalented husband, John, live in the village funeral home. I discovered Celia was indeed a Christian, an independent thinker, and an ambitious writer as well.

Now Celia is publishing a book. In addition to telling you what it's like to live in a funeral home, pursuing an ancient and altogether necessary profession, she will tell you stories sliced with bright insight, and, in a series of appendices, hand you useful information as well—information about funerals that, inevitably, we will all need to know.

But the best pages in her book are pages that introduce you to Celia herself. Celia is not afraid to be Celia. She has opinions, and she will tell you what she believes. Naturally, she will promote what I suppose might be termed "a full service funeral," but you wouldn't expect anything else, would you?

Much more, Celia will tell you of her growing up on a family farm, of finding her way through different jobs, always learning, and finally of a long commute to complete her advanced theological education. Of course, she will tell you of life in a small, Midwestern American village. And, yes, she will tell stories of what it's like to be a family in a funeral home. Some of her stories are just "good stories," some are astonishing, and some will move in your mind quite wonderfully. What's the best thing about the book? Getting to know Celia and her on-call, splendid faith in the eternal Living God. So come, read the pages—Celia will tell you who she is.

I have a summertime cottage on a little lake not far from the village where Celia and John Hastings live. Now every summer I look forward to greeting them again. But this summer my wife and I hope to celebrate with them the publication of *The Undertaker's Wife.*

David Buttrick
Drucilla Moore Buffington Professor
of Homiletics and Liturgics, Emeritus
Vanderbilt University

W e all eventually reach a time in life when we can view from the vantage point of past years how the pieces of the puzzle of our lives come together. We can look back on our different choices, the people we've known, the joys and sorrows, the smooth and bumpy roads, and the opportunities seized or lost. Rather than being randomly threaded throughout the years, we see how they have been sewn together to form the pattern of our life. If we are wise, we also see how our experiences are life lessons.

Busy on the journey of life, we seldom find time to stop to consider where we've been or where we're going. In telling her life story, Celia Hastings compels us to stop. Her stories are life lessons. By recalling her years of growing up on a farm, she takes us back to the sweet and simple pleasures of life, of lessons learned in a rural schoolhouse, in the fields picking strawberries, and feeding chickens. The future was as wide open as the fields of corn and distant as the horizon.

In her stories as an undertaker's wife, she also compels us to stop and contemplate the meaning of having lived life. She shares captivating stories about a potpourri of people and pets ranging from her Great Aunt Tillie to Ms. Kitty the cat. In her testimony of faith, she reminds us of the true meaning of life and reassures us of the promise of eternal life.

Each of her stops along the way is another piece of the puzzle, another thread in her life quilt, and another life lesson. The farm girl from the open country who finds herself in the fishbowl of a small-town undertaker's business uses her life experience to examine the meaning of life, death, God, and life after death.

Today's life journey is fast-paced and busy. We have at our disposal an increasing number of gadgets and conveniences that with each passing year become quicker and more portable. We have an overload of media competing for our attention. We multitask, and microwave, and juggle. Our food is fast and our electronic mail instant. Little time is left to learn from experience or contemplate existence.

Celia happens to be my second cousin. My parents and I visited the farm she describes in this book every summer for several years. It's fascinating how growing up on that farm shaped Celia for the rest of her life. Talk about multitasking! Just reading about her long chore list of picking, hoeing, feeding, hauling, gathering, and harvesting is exhausting. Yet, the work was its own reward in preparing her for the twists and turns of life and in contemplating life itself. Every experience, from the work of harvesting corn and gathering eggs to the joys of playing in the barn and visiting with relatives, shaped the adult she would become.

Few people today have the opportunity to grow up on a farm. But we *can* discover that place in our hearts where we can find the time to contemplate, to consider the lessons of our lives, and to seek answers about the important questions that go beyond day-to-day living.

As an undertaker's wife, much of Celia's life revolved around the end of life's journey. Through contemplation and understanding, that experience became life affirming. In the midst of dying, she learns that life is a gift. She encourages us to celebrate life. And yet, she reassures us that, with faith in Jesus Christ, we need not fear death.

It's been a pleasure to pause and reflect on Celia's life lessons and be reminded of the lessons from my own life journey. I hope that many others will take the time to stop long enough in their life journeys to reflect on her wisdom and appreciate the gift of life.

Helen DeVos
Richard and Helen DeVos Foundation

Preface

"**Y**ou should write a book," people would often tell me. I was never sure if they thought that living in a small-town funeral home was a unique experience that would make for a good book or whether it was a polite way to dismiss the topic of death and funerals.

If it was the latter, I certainly understand. Death and funerals are topics many people prefer to avoid. Including me. Living in a small-town funeral home was nothing I chose or planned. It's just the way life unfolded for me.

My discomfort with funeral service was obvious to John and his family while we were dating. One night as we were returning from a movie in the family station wagon, it stalled and wouldn't start again (really!). We hitchhiked into town, and he went to get the family's only other vehicle—*the hearse*—to take me home. But I refused to ride in it saying, "It isn't my time yet." (I was remembering a few years earlier when my grandpa had died suddenly in a doctor's office and had ridden in *that hearse*.)

John's father tried to sway me. "It's just a vehicle," he cajoled. Well it may have been *just a vehicle* to them, but it meant something else to me, and I had no intention of riding in it! John and his dad conferred privately. They resorted to borrowing a car from the local used car dealer so that John could take me home.

My discomfort with funerals also showed itself a year later when my grandmother died and I wouldn't go to the visitation because I didn't want to see her in her casket. I had a reason: Grandma's hair. She had always washed her long hair in rainwater gathered in outdoor buckets and stored in her bathtub. I can still picture her brushing one hundred strokes every morning—back to front, left to right, right to left, and front to back. Then she wound and pinned her hair into a labyrinthine crown. But when she went into the nursing home they cut her hair, permed it, and said, "Now doesn't that look nice?" I remembered how sheepish and humiliated she had looked the first time I saw her after the cut and perm. The way Grandma took care of her hair had always been so much a part of her that I knew there was no way she could look "just like herself" in a casket. I attended her funeral, but my refusal to look at Grandma in her casket was seen by my family as disrespectful and by John's family as "immature."

So I wasn't "a natural" for funeral service; but it didn't matter, because, when we married, John was in the Air Force and planning a career in engineering. Life, however, took both of us through many unexpected twists and turns. Within ten years of our wedding, the sergeant I married had become a funeral director in charge of the family business. I learned to do paperwork, play the organ, officiate, and sometimes even drive *the hearse.*

Acknowledgments

I am grateful to Dirk Wierenga, Louann Werksma, and Ginny McFadden of FaithWalk Publishing for asking me to write this book and shepherding it into existence.

I gratefully acknowledge all those who have been my teachers in the university of life and college of experience. My sincere thanks to all whose stories, conversations, and wisdom have directly or indirectly shaped this book. Names and details have been changed to protect personal privacy.

Introduction

It is better to go to the house of mourning
than to go to the house of feasting ...
Sorrow is better than laughter:
for by the sadness of the countenance the heart is made better.
Ecclesiastes 7:2–3, KJV

Y ou never could have convinced me that "Sorrow is better
than laughter" when I was younger. I much preferred to
laugh. But many years of living in a small-town funeral home
have borne out the truth of this proverb. I've watched many
families weave the wisdom of their loved ones into their own
lives by sharing sadness and hugs, pictures and stories, thereby
strengthening family and community. As grief is released and
happy memories are recalled, often laughter abounds as well
as tears in the house of mourning.

The author of this proverb concluded that much of life
amounted to meaningless chasing after the wind. But the
house of mourning is a good place to sit with the Teacher, to
listen and learn what's really important in life.

In the house of mourning I've put into practice a key
concept taught me long ago by an elderly teacher: "If you
know how to read, you can learn anything." And the discern-
ing observation of a farmer: "You can tell a lot about people
by the way they treat animals."

Small-town funeral homes such as ours used to outnum-
ber larger ones and were an important part of community life.
But in the past fifty years many funeral homes have combined

or merged according to the bigger-is-better theory. It seemed small-town funeral homes, like family farms and country schools, were going the way of the dinosaur.

Some trends give us hope, however: "new urban" city planning and architecture, with a focus on restoring human-scale, "walkable" communities; small farmers coalescing into community-based cooperatives; and the factory model of public education giving way to more individualized learning and home schooling. Perhaps small-town funeral homes will survive into the future rather than simply fade into the past.

In these pages I share the stories of day-to-day life inside a small-town funeral home, sprinkled with reflections on life, death, Scripture, and faith, as well as practical information about making funeral arrangements, planning a funeral or memorial service, and questions for personal journaling or discussion. It is my hope that this book will provide a light-hearted glimpse inside a way of life you've never thought much about; and, while you laugh at our adventures, perhaps you'll also learn from the people you meet in these pages how to meet grief, loss, and death—your own or someone else's—without fear.

(If you've picked up this book for an immediate need, you may find it helpful to go to the flow chart, Appendix A, and other appendices at the back of the book.)

One

How Did I Arrive at a Place Like This?

We live our lives forward,
but we understand them backward.
Soren Kierkegaard (1813–1855)

I live in a funeral home. Not above it or beside it. Right in it. It isn't anything I ever planned or dreamed of doing. There was no training program to prepare me for living here, but I've learned the ropes and come to love a life that most people would never even consider.

I was raised nearby on a small family farm. My parents also had grown up on family farms and were educated in one-room country schools; my mom later taught in those schools. On the farm my older sister, younger brother, and I learned many skills—feeding calves and chickens; gathering and washing eggs; hoeing the garden and the corn; picking beans for the local canning factory; picking cherries, straw-berries, raspberries, and potatoes; helping to haul hay and har-vest corn and oats.

We also had fun. We climbed trees, built forts, and made daily rounds to check birds' nests. One summer my sister and I transformed an old covered corn crib into a doll house. But instead of filling it with dolls, we caught kittens from a neighbor's barn, named them, tamed them, and played with them in the corncrib/dollhouse. We dubbed it our "cat house." The kittens played tag, climbing and swinging on an old blanket we hung across the middle of the corncrib. Pandy became a "shoulder cat" and clung there even when I rode my bike. Trixie allowed us to dress her in doll clothes and push her around in a doll buggy.

That summer Trixie died. We had a funeral and buried her, returning her to the earth the best we could. A few weeks later we noticed her tail was sticking out. Dad helped us with a disinterment and a more dignified reinterment.

When our "city-slicker" cousins visited the farm during the summer, we took them to Trixie's grave, then showed them around our cat house, wondering why they found this so amusing.

Continuing our role as tour guides, we country hicks moved the focus of the tour to the barnyard. These were the days when our dairy herd was in transition from Guernsey and Jersey cows (whose milk was rich in butterfat for making cream) to Holsteins (who gave greater volume for producing Grade A milk). We told our cousins that Guernseys and Jerseys gave butter and cheese while Holsteins gave skim milk and chocolate milk. They wondered how this could be—until their mom, who used to milk cows, told them how butter and cheese were made.

Music Lessons for Milk

When we weren't giving barnyard tours, we acquired a bit of culture right in our own neighborhood. Mrs. Taylor was a neighbor who had been a concert pianist before suffering a diabetic stroke that paralyzed her left hand. She cried for three days. Then she figured out a way she could still enjoy music: teaching others to play. She recruited us, and we took piano lessons on the barter system. For each lesson we carried four quart jars of fresh skim milk in a wire carrier up the hill to her home. She drank it, still warm. We grimaced. She said it made "new blood within twenty minutes." While she was building her blood we were reshaping our hands from gripping the handle of the wire carrier. When everyone was ready, we performed scales, arpeggios, and songs as she directed and sang along. She demonstrated both the treble and bass parts of new pieces with her right hand, but she kept exercising her left hand, proudly demonstrating each measurable gain. In time she was able to play octaves and chords with her left hand, showing us that persistence pays. She even held a recital for us in her small home—as part of a neighborhood Halloween party. After our rousing performance we bobbed for apples and ate popcorn balls.

In spite of a confining farm schedule our lives were enriched by many relatives who visited the farm. With our cousins we played hide-and-seek in the hay mow and corn field, built forts in the hay mow, shared family stories and jokes, took day trips, and listened in on the grownups' political and theological discussions.

An Adventure "Out East"

Life on a farm doesn't lend itself well to family vacations, but the summer when I was twelve and my sister thirteen, our 72-year-old great Aunt Tillie came for a visit and, after two weeks, she took us girls "back east" to visit her siblings and their families. They were the eight children of a parson and his wife, and several had become ministers, too. Our grandmother had died when we were babies, and I suspect Aunt Tillie was playing grandmother. She drove us in her 1956

Ford, first to Grand Rapids, then through Canada to Williamson, New York, and on to Binghamton, where she lived. We stayed in her three-story house, which featured a dramatic, winding staircase and pulley-driven clotheslines between her house and the carriage house in back.

It took a week to fully explore the place with its Tiffany lamps, Persian rugs, grand piano, and reed organ. We helped her with some cleaning tasks and ate meals in the breakfast nook, at the kitchen table, and in the dining room. We entertained Aunt Tillie by playing her piano and organ. She took us by train (and relatives' cars) to East Orange, Creskill, and Wayne, New Jersey, and by boat to Staten Island where we saw the Statue of Liberty across the harbor. In New Jersey we enjoyed picnics with relatives, and it was our cousins' turn to play tour guide. They borrowed a convertible and took us through the Lincoln Tunnel, over the George Washington Bridge, and in and around New York City.

Since our four great uncles were pastors (two were also authors), we stayed in parsonages; ate formal dinners in their dining rooms; visited their churches; and listened to sermons, theological discussions, and more family stories before returning to Binghamton by train.

After three weeks, we realized we had worn proper dresses and exhibited "company manners" for far too long. We longed for the wide open spaces and casual freedom of the farm. We missed our pets and, of course, our own ministry of barnyard tours. Not wanting to hurt Aunt Tillie's feelings, we walked the bridge over the Susquehanna River, found a pay phone, and called home collect. Aunt Tillie smiled knowingly when we returned and said, "I'm so glad you could come, but I know it has been a long time for you." She packed muffins, sandwiches, chips, apples, grapes, and bananas and put us on the train back to northern Michigan, generously tipping the conductor to ensure our safe transfer in Buffalo at midnight.

In the year following this trip, I started high school. One of my thirty-five classmates was John, class president and the son of our town's only funeral director. After four years of studies, class parties, and fundraisers, we all embarked on our senior class trip to New York City—by bus. Just before the trip John invited me for a ride on his homemade vehicle, Chug-a-lug, and to his surprise I accepted.

Soon after graduation, I left for the summer term at a business college four hours from home. One weekend when I was home, John invited me for a ride in his newly acquired 1930 Model A Ford, and to his surprise I accepted. Later, to check out whether this might be true love, I asked if I could drive the Model A, and to *my* surprise *he* consented—on the condition that I learn to double-clutch (which I did!).

This was during the Vietnam War. John had attended college for a year after high school but had run out of funds, and the draft board was breathing down his neck. He enlisted in the U.S. Air Force, hoping to get training in mechanics or engineering—something which might be useful in civilian life. After undergoing the USAF's highly personalized career and psychological screening, John was placed in "munitions and weapons" and sent to Guam for eighteen months. We exchanged letters. In one he wrote: "Even though President Nixon says the war is de-escalating, we are loading just as many bombs onto just as many B52s, and I don't think they're dropping them in the ocean."

Road Trip West

While John was serving in Guam (aka, "The Rock"), I roomed with my friend Jan, a hairdresser who taught me a few basic styling skills. But soon Jan and I decided to see the U.S.A. in my Chevrolet. We left northern Michigan on January 6, 1969.

There were six inches of fluffy snow on the ground and snow was falling as we left, but we figured we'd drive out of it as we headed south. My trusty 1964 Chevy was loaded with everything we owned—stereo, typewriter, sewing machine, and clothing. Jan and I each had $100 for our travels.

By the time we reached I-80, the fluffy snow of northern Michigan had become a major blizzard. In spite of travelers' warnings and semi-trucks overturned in the median, we kept traveling because we were on a tight budget. We switched drivers often to prevent snow blindness, stayed overnight in Iowa, and arrived in Denver amid tornado-strength winds the following evening.

After staying with my aunt for a week, we found an apartment and jobs—Jan as a bank loan officer and I as research secretary at a university. As I did research in the library and typed and retyped manuscripts, I learned the process of publication: research, write, edit, rewrite, edit, submit to journals, edit galley proofs, and finally see the article published in a professional journal.

Each day in Denver provided a view of the majestic Rocky Mountains and the healthful benefits of the arid, mile-high climate. I enjoyed skiing with a university group and camping with a church career group. Soon John's tour on Guam was completed. While he was in flight from Guam to Denver he watched live coverage of the astronauts' first landing on the moon. I watched the moon landing from the university's big screen, then met John at the airport. We discovered that our love had survived the long separation, so we made wedding plans. We were married on September 27, 1969.

Our first home was in Wichita where John worked for the Strategic Air Command (SAC) at McConnell Air Force Base and I did medical, legal, and corporate office work through a temp agency. John's work meant he was often on call. This was before pagers and cell phones, so whenever we were away from our home phone, he had to call SAC and give a number where he could be reached. Once we were at a couples' party when he got called out, and I was stranded—my first taste of being suddenly single. (Little did I know how many times this would happen in the years to come.)

When John was discharged early for education, we moved back to Michigan where he studied electronics technology and steam-cleaned carpets. But when he graduated from college the electronics industry was in a slump and there were no jobs. So he continued cleaning carpets. Then came the energy crisis of the 1970s, and his hours were cut. Meanwhile John's father, who was past sixty-five, said, "I can't afford to retire unless you take over the business. If you get your license, I'll make you a good deal."

Off we went downstate, with our 3-year-old son, Paul. While John studied and worked in a funeral home I did medical transcription in our home. John read anatomy and embalming textbooks; I reread *Daddy Was an Undertaker,*[1] which was required reading for anyone marrying into John's family. It's the story of a young girl growing up above a small-town funeral home with a mother who insisted her children call home whenever they heard police or fire sirens.

Personal Losses

Through our reading and conversations, John and I became aware that our views of death and grief were quite different. In John's family death was a natural part of life, nothing to get excited about. In my family death and grief were complex issues. Although we often dealt with the death of farm animals and pets, my family had some not-fully-processed grief experiences which permeated all of life and made each loss more difficult. This was obvious to me during a family reunion at a lake when my aunts frantically insisted everyone wear a life jacket, even though we were wading in shallow water. The looks of horror on their faces recalled the time their 33-year-old brother had drowned while swimming during a family 4th of July picnic despite my dad's and uncles' attempts to rescue him. My uncle left a widow and 6-year-old son.

My paternal grandfather had died of pancreatic cancer when Dad was nine, leaving Grandma to raise six children. As soon as her daughters completed eighth grade, Grandma sent them to work as housekeepers in far-flung cities—with instructions to send half their pay home to help her raise the rest of the children, which they did! In spite of being a widow's only son at home, my dad was drafted in World War II, drove an ammo truck, built bridges in Europe, was in the D-Day battle, and drove through the death camps. This was before post-traumatic stress disorder was named or understood. My parents were married in Chicago as soon as Dad was discharged.

In Mom's family, there was the loss of a baby brother when she was twelve. Then, when she was a young adult, her mother died of a blood clot following surgery. So while death was "natural" to John and his family, it meant tragedy, hardship, and lingering sadness in mine.

After John's graduation and state and national board exams, we moved back to our hometown and bought the funeral home. For the next ten years we lived in rented houses while his folks continued to live in the funeral home. When his Dad was ill and needed more peace and quiet, his folks moved out. With our son Paul, who was entering his high school years, we moved in.

While I adjusted from my former life in a small house beside a quiet stream to fishbowl living arrangements, John began some remodeling projects: tearing out old plaster and lath, rewiring, drywalling, painting. I worked with him at funerals, passing out folders, playing organ preludes and postludes, accompanying soloists, and transcribing funeral messages from audio recordings as a gift to the families we served, continuing the tradition that John's mom had begun of taking sermon notes and hand copying them into memory books, but with a modern twist.

Commuting to Seminary

For many years it seemed I lived life from day to day without any goals or plans, but after I had spent years in Bible study and teaching, two pastors I knew observed I was "searching for something" and suggested I might find it at seminary. There was an immediate opening at Western Theological Seminary in Holland, Michigan, for a student with an associate's degree, so I enrolled. For the next three years I drove the 400 mile round trip once a week, staying overnight with one of my great uncles, a widowed and retired pastor, who lived near the seminary. For my cross-cultural study unit, I received a scholarship for a two-week study tour of Israel, which took place just before the Persian Gulf War. After graduating from the same seminary as my great-grandfather and four great uncles, I served as an interim pastor, officiated at funerals upon request, and began writing a Bible survey course for adults.

While at first glance a farm kid with grief baggage and a kid who grew up in a funeral home but liked mechanics might seem an unlikely combination for mom-and-pop funeral service, a look backward shows that, little by little, we were both being prepared. Both of us grew up in self-employed families with 24/7 responsibilities—even our wedding had to be planned around funerals and the cows' milking schedule. John had his own lawn-mowing business and was accustomed to augmenting his income with part-time work, a necessity for a small-town funeral director who doesn't want to starve. He could be flexibile in his schedule and readily accepted the responsibility of community service. From his hobbies he had learned vehicle maintenance and carpentry skills. After serving in the Air Force and working for another funeral director he realized he preferred self-employment. When preparation met opportunity, he welcomed the life of a small-town undertaker, and I became the undertaker's wife.

Looking back I realize that, although I'd had no formal training, much of my life prepared me for what I now do. The solitude of country living and caring for animals resonates through the Twenty-third Psalm—a favorite at funerals. Those early neighborhood piano lessons (and lots of practice) eventually enabled me to play at funerals. Living with a hairdresser provided tips which were useful in preparing bodies for viewing. Travel with Aunt Tillie connected me with my heritage of pastors and authors and provided a backdrop for seminary training, writing a Bible study, and officiating at funerals. Business training familiarized me with office work and the medical terminology used on death certificates. Working as a transcriptionist prepared me for transcribing funeral messages as a gift to families we serve, which in turn taught me much about theology and message preparation. Consorting with the funeral director's kid eventually landed me in a small-town funeral home. Reading funeral and grief books sensitized me to my own views on death and grief and how they were formed (and reformed) and made me more understaning of the grief experiences of others.

Indeed, it appears I was being prepared all along.

Afterthoughts

1. The life of Jacob, the ancient shepherd, went through many ironic twists and turns. At the end of his life he looked back and said, "God … has been my shepherd all my life to this day." (Gn 48:15, NRSV) How may God be shepherding you little by little, bit by bit, stage by stage, step by step, day by day?

2. What does Kierkegaard's statement, "We live our lives forward, but we understand them backward" mean in your life?

Recommended Reading

1. Hagberg, Janet O. *Real Power: Stages of Personal Power in Organizations.* Salem: Sheffield Publishing Company, 1994, 1984.

2. Sheehy, Gail. *Passages: Predictable Crises of Adult Life.* E.P. Dutton & Company, Inc., 1974, 1976.

3. Viorst, Judith. *Necessary Losses: The Loves, Illusions, Dependencies, and Impossible Expectations That All of Us Have to Give Up in Order to Grow,* New York: Fireside, 1986, first Fireside Edition, 1998.

Two

What's It Like to Live in a Funeral Home?

"If you can't do something the way it should be done,
do it the way it can be done."

Tena Drenth Bolhuis
(my paternal Grandma)

"Two phones, a doorbell, and a one-track mind" is the way I often describe my daily life.

We live in the center of town, a stone's throw from the four corners, next to the post office and across the street from the restaurant, which makes it easy for people to stop by to pre-plan a funeral, order a monument or marker, ask about a cemetery plot, do genealogical research, or reserve a date at the community hall (where John is custodian). Add sales reps and deliveries besides visitations and funerals, and, well, you get the picture.

Our home/funeral home is a 100-year-old white frame structure with a brick front and glass door. Next door is the post office—which also has a brick front and glass door. Sometimes people absentmindedly come through our front door to mail a package or buy stamps. (Even the postmaster did it once.) Inside our place, besides the chapel, are rooms that each serve several purposes. The dining room doubles as an office, the kitchen as a coffee room, and the living room as a children's play room when needed. With chairs set up in the living room, dining room (with the table rolled into the den), and chapel we can seat ninety people. A sound system reaches all rooms.

Besides the post office, funeral home, and restaurant, our town boasts a used car lot, a couple of service stations, a photography and gift shop, a party store, a tavern, a farmers co-op, a fire station, a public school with an enrollment of about 250 students in grades kindergarten through twelve, a private elementary school with thirty students, a trucking firm, and a pallet mill. Many village residents work out of town.

When a family needs a funeral director, they may choose to have John come to their home, or they may come in and make arrangements around our dining room table. During the family interview, John obtains the information needed for the certificate of death and obituary. The other services we perform depend upon the family's choice of the method of disposition: burial, cremation, entombment, or donation (*see Appendix D*). For the convenience of the family, a clergy person sometimes meets with them at the funeral home to plan the service.

Usually we serve one family at a time. When there are more, visitations and services are scheduled so that each family has full use of the facilities. During especially busy times, funeral directors in nearby towns assist as needed.

Our in-house division of labor is what you might expect of a mom-and-pop outfit. John does the "body work" (except for women's hair styling, which I usually do), and I do much of the paperwork. I type obituaries and transmit them by fax or e-mail—which is much easier than how we did it when we first started, calling them in to the newspapers and spelling every name and place. I type death certificates, obtain doctors' signatures, and file them with the clerk in the county in which the death occurred. Cremation requires the authorization of the medical examiner as well, and most charge a fee for this, which is collected at the county clerk's office. Cremation also requires written authorization of the next of kin. If several persons are equally next of kin—such as children or siblings—all must sign, or a reasonable effort must be made to obtain all signatures. Faxed signatures are acceptable.

Multitasking to Make Ends Meet

Each day, John and I weave funeral service with other daily tasks. He drives the school bus and does custodial work at the community hall as well as home maintenance, lawn mowing in the summer, and snow shoveling in the winter. He serves on the local fire and rescue department, Veterans Trust Fund, and American Legion. Meanwhile I cook, bake, clean, do laundry, transport friends and relatives to medical appointments, make hospital calls and home visits upon request, officiate at funerals for other funeral homes, officiate at weddings, and work on community projects such as building a labyrinth and sensory garden.

As you can imagine, preparing meals and eating during busy times can be challenging. We sometimes eat in shifts or get takeout food from the local restaurant or bar. For many years we had a grocery store nearby, but that eventually became a party store; the nearest grocery store is now six miles away. Years ago I developed allergies to corn and wheat, which meant I had to know what was in my food, read labels, adapt recipes, discover new foods—such as spelt (an ancient grain similar to wheat)—or select carefully from menus. I try to keep a well stocked freezer as well as other foods that can be quickly prepared: peanut butter toast, muffins, scrambled eggs, baked potatoes, veggies for steaming. For many years we've kept a small garden of rhubarb, carrots, beets, beans, tomatoes, radishes, and onions. John plants and tills. I harvest, bake, can, and freeze.

Besides finding time to eat, getting enough sleep can be challenging also. While many nights we sleep in heavenly peace, other nights the fire and rescue monitor goes off or the phone rings to notify us that someone has died. To get everything done we may have to work late at night or get up early in the morning. We know we're exhausted when we feel a twinge of envy for the person in the casket.

During not-so-busy times we enjoy hobbies. John restores reed organs, traveling to monthly workshops during the warmer months. He enjoys auctions, tinkering with his Model A and Model T, and fishing. I enjoy reading, writing, playing piano and organ, doing jigsaw puzzles, listening to music, and attending spiritual workshops and retreats. Sometimes our work and hobbies fit together well; at other times it's a complicated juggling act and results in our having to forego planned events.

Flexibility First and Foremost

When we first moved back to our hometown and John's folks were living in the funeral home, there was some wiggle room in scheduling, and we actually made plans and carried them out! However, there were other times we had to cancel dinner dates, social events, and meetings at the last minute. Sometimes it seemed, "If it weren't for funerals, we'd have no social life at all." The other side of our unpredictable schedule is that we get to meet people we wouldn't otherwise have met, share common interests and ideas, and see people we haven't seen in awhile. As the second generation in family funeral service, our work can be more meaningful because we've known many of the people we serve for a long time;

however, this can also make our work more emotionally difficult. Often it feels like we're burying family.

The inability to plan our lives was at times difficult for me because I grew up on a dairy farm where cows had to be milked twice a day on a regular schedule. This meant mealtimes had to be regular, and we all sat at the table together. Adapting to an irregular working, eating, sleeping, and social life was a stretch for me. Little by little I learned to lay aside plans on short notice, to attend events without John, to "seize the day," enjoy individual pursuits, and savor solitude as well as impromptu social gatherings.

John's parents had also learned to juggle an unpredictable schedule when they first came to Ellsworth in 1942. John's dad had worked at another funeral home where, as the employee, he had to do all the night and weekend work. A sales rep told him about a small town that needed a funeral director, so in 1942 they traveled there with a baby, a 1937 Oldsmobile hearse/ambulance combination called a "duplex," and thirty-five dollars in cash, which they used to rent an apartment.

Local Citizen Gets into Jam

When they bought the old house (which was actually two old houses put together in a T-shape) for a funeral home, a local resident loaned them the money because the community wanted a locally owned funeral home. For many years their only vehicle was the Olds duplex, but they eventually bought a 1947 Cadillac duplex, which they used well into the 1960s. It had a flip-up, rear-facing seat for an attendant (usually a family member) if one was available. The duplex was a practical way for a small town to have both ambulance and funeral service.

Of the many emergencies the duplexes tended, one run became a legend. There was a car-pedestrian accident one night, and the pedestrian appeared badly injured, with blood everywhere. After they got him to the hospital and started removing his clothes they discovered he had a jar of strawberry jelly in his back pocket. Crushed in the accident, it was the source of the "blood."

John's dad estimated that about 10 percent of the ambulance runs were for medical emergencies and 90 percent were for accidents that involved alcohol. After each run, the ambulance had to be cleaned, badly soiled sheets had to be laundered and ironed, and many clients never paid; so no one in small town funeral service was sorry when ambulance service was taken over by local government.

Being "outsiders" to this Dutch-American community, John's parents had to learn "the way we do things around here." For women this meant "vash on Monday, iron on Tuesday, bake on Vensday, mend on Tursday, clean on Friday, and on Saturday polish shoes, get meals ready for Sunday ven ve go to church and do no verk." Elderly women in the community wore hats, even to the grocery store. One day Gertie walked past the funeral home on Wednesday and saw sheets and diapers hanging on the clothesline on the front porch. She scolded John's mom, "You vash on *Vensday*?" Mom replied, "Well it was rainy and windy Monday, and I thought the sheets would blow up against the siding of the house and get dirty." Gertie replied, "Vell! I *vash* my clapboard!"

When John's parents arrived in the village the state-of-the-art communication tool was an old crank wall phone, and their "answering service" was the local telephone operator who always knew where to reach them. Later they had an off-premise extension. Forty-four years later, at the time of their retirement, they had progressed to an answering ma-

chine, programming it each time they left with a number
where they could be reached.

The house had only one bathroom, without tub or shower, until they took out a mortgage and did extensive remodeling in the 1960s. Because they had invested so much in the
business, the only way they could afford retirement was if we
bought the business while they continued to live there. These
living arrangements were part of the terms of purchase.

Hometown Homesteaders

We were used to moving around and had lived in a variety
of places—a small apartment during Air Force years, a rented
trailer when John was in college and Paul was born, an older
home we bought and remodeled, a HUD housing complex
during mortuary school years—so, after buying the funeral home, we rented a nearby house for two years until the
owners retired and wanted their house back. To temporarily
cover cracked kitchen linoleum, I bought a wild-print, or-
ange-burgundy-yellow-black carpet for twenty-seven dollars.
John stapled it down and we enjoyed it for two years, but if
you dropped a piece of tomato on it you'd never find it. We
thought the owners would soon replace the kitchen carpet,
but they loved the splash of bright color, and it remains to this
day, as does our friendship.

For the next eight years we rented a bungalow on the
edge of town. Although a family had raised ten children in
this three-bedroom home, the three of us didn't have enough
closet space for seasonal clothing. So John built a frame around
the top of an expandable clothes rack, and I covered it with
fabric and curtained it to form a "closet." He learned to repair
things that otherwise might have ended up in a landfill, and as

a result we have lamps, dressers, antique oak chairs, and even a round oak table. Our credo was "make do, redo, or do without" or "improvise, invent, repair." And when our improvisations were not so useful, they were at least entertaining.

Although there was an oil furnace in the bungalow, John added a wood-burning furnace for cozy and economical heat. We cut, split, and stacked our own wood, hauling it from the woods with a small trailer pulled by an orchard tractor we had acquired as part payment from an insolvent estate. John ran a loop of copper pipe into the furnace and connected it to the electric hot water heater, an arrangement that generated more hot water than we could use. "Someone take a bath or shower!" or "Run a load of laundry in hot water!" we'd say when we heard water coming from the overflow pipe. The copper loop arrangement cut our electric bill in half.

With a woodpile beside the house, the tricolored, partially-restored Model A Ford beside the woodpile, and the old John Deere orchard tractor we used for hauling wood, our place became a tourist attraction, with people often stopping by to ask if the car or tractor were for sale. Once someone asked to buy the Model A for a "parts car." When I told that to John he walked around for three days saying, "*Parts car.* They want *my car* for a *parts car!* It *has* all its parts." On the third day, he taped the windows and bumpers, and spray painted the whole car black. After its more unified look no one ever again asked to buy it for a parts car.

While many people enjoyed restoring old cars for show, we enjoyed taking ours on back country roads and two-tracks, watching deer and wild turkeys along the way. We went morel mushrooming each year, stopping to visit a woodsman friend who could stack wood so well you couldn't see daylight through the pile. When we bought a cord of wood from him, it was really a cord-and-a-half.

Since the bungalow was on a spacious lot, we had a big garden with rhubarb, corn, strawberries, pole beans, potatoes, tomatoes, cucumbers, squash, carrots, onions, and beets. Besides our own produce, I canned applesauce, peaches, plums, and cherries from nearby orchards.

Culinary Adventures

Although I hadn't spent a lot of time in the kitchen when I was growing up, I learned how to make many of our meals from scratch. For a few years I made pizza and antipasto salad every Saturday night. Sometimes sales reps and friends arrived at dinnertime and joined us for sandwiches with homemade bread still warm from the oven, turkey, and provolone cheese. Other times city-slicker cousins arrived at dinnertime in late summer. I dug potatoes from the garden, picked beans, pulled some carrots, and while they were cooking fired up the hibachi and grilled some burgers. Their response to my pioneer-woman performance was, "Do you have any cherry pie?" So for a grand finale I would spread rusk (crisp toasted biscuits) with canned cherry pie filling and whipped topping.

During long winter "cabin-fever seasons" I conducted scientific experiments (or "culinary rituals") in the kitchen, learning new skills via the trial-and-error method. One winter it was gelatin, another breadmaking, and eventually chocolate fudge. I wanted an old-fashioned chocolate fudge, not the too-sweet marshmallow-and-chocolate chip kind. Fudge had always been difficult for me to make without burning it. I had tried a candy thermometer without success. Since microwaves act on sugar and liquids, I decided to try that, hoping it wouldn't burn. I used a large deep bowl (because it foams), experimented with proportions, different kinds of chocolate, and learned cold-water testing. This experimentation eventually produced a decadent, melt-in-your-mouth chocolate fudge. Meanwhile we all had fun eating my less successful experiments with spoons.

Celia's "Old-Fashioned" Microwave Fudge

4 ounces unsweetened chocolate
(Belgian or Swiss is best)
4 cups sugar
1 (12 ounce) can evaporated milk
½ teaspoon salt

Place in large bowl, stir, and microwave approximately 20 minutes on high, stirring every few minutes until it forms a soft ball in cold water. Then add:

8 ounces good-quality margarine
1 ½ Tablespoons vanilla
Beat with electric mixer five minutes or more until mixture thickens and loses its gloss. Pour into a greased 8"x 8" glass pan.

While cooking remains more of a survival skill than a forté for me, when John was our town's fire chief and a family lost their house to a fire, the local fire chief's wife was "expected" to organize a benefit dinner. I made many calls trying to get someone with better food preparation and organizational skills to head up the project. Everyone said they'd help, but no one wanted to take charge. Thankfully, everyone I contacted volunteered something: salads, rolls, desserts, and even the main course. That's when I realized that the meal was self-organizing, and called them all back and said, "You're on." When it was announced at the local softball field that I was heading up a benefit dinner, everyone knew it was a shaky situation and came forward to help. The result was a success-ful fundraiser dinner, and I had the privilege of presenting a check to the family to help with their immediate needs.

While living in the bungalow, we gradually assumed more and more tasks of the business while John's folks continued to live in the funeral home, travel and enjoy their retirement years. As we made changes, John says his dad had to bite his tongue a lot. His mom bristled a bit as I took over the task of preparing memory books because I transcribed the funeral messages from a tape rather than outlining by hand and writ-ing them as she had done. "I guess the way I did things wasn't good enough," she'd say. When I helped John move the casket to the front of the church at the beginning of the service, his dad had reservations about a woman doing that in a conser-vative community; but since I was able, available, and worked cheap, the practice continued.

Friendships Fostered in Losses Shared

During our first few years in the business, books on the topic of grief and dying began to roll off the presses with greater regularity, following the success of Elizabeth Kuebler-Ross's *On Death And Dying,*[1] which was the standard while John was in training. John and I read many and built a small library. My mother-in-law, who sometimes scorned "intellectuals" who weren't as practical as she, volunteered this wisdom: "Celia, there are things in life that are worse than death."

Still, I saw a lot of loneliness among widows in the com-munity and invited them to our home for an afternoon. They stayed for three hours, drinking coffee, playing games, visiting, making and renewing friendships. A local widows' support group was born. Monthly meetings were planned around information the women wanted, such as handling finances, estate planning, fire safety, home maintenance, auto maintenance and repair. One woman didn't know how to put gas in her car. Another took drivers' training when she was in her sixties. "Got it up to forty the other day," she'd brag with a twinkle in her eye.

Word spread around town, and soon local widowers came to me: "You should organize a group for the men, too. It's harder for them." So one evening I invited several widowers to come to our home for dinner and a meeting with John and a social worker. I made a dinner of roast beef, mashed potatoes and gravy, corn, beans, and cherry crisp. Although I didn't consider myself homemaker-of-the-year material, men who had been living on canned soup and beef stew gave my efforts rave reviews.

Both groups continued for a couple of years until the local seniors' group launched similar programs. Widowed men and women now realized they had the power to help each other. Our county obtained a grant for a widow-to-widow program in a rural area, and the need for support was filled in a new way. Later, hospice organizations became active in our area, offering grief support to clients and non-clients.

From our groups emerged a love story. Ethan retired to have more time to care for his invalid wife, but she died a few weeks after he retired, which gave Ethan the twin loss of widowhood and retirement. He became depressed, and his family was quite concerned about him. So were we, until one evening, at one of our group meetings he took John aside, told him he had known one of the widows many years before when they worked at the same place, and wanted to contact her but didn't know where she was living. He asked John to get her address and phone number from the widows' list and slip it to him.

As a gentleman, Ethan wouldn't use the secret information until Barbara had passed the first anniversary of her husband's death. A few weeks later his family noticed changes in
him. Ethan's perplexed niece said, "Something's changed. I
don't know why, but he's painting the house and says the sun
is starting to shine in his life again." After a couple of weeks
the secret was out. Ethan and Barbara made plans together,
visited each of their adult children, and explained, "We're not
trying to replace the parent you lost, just trying to make the
best of what is."

The widowers' group held a bachelor party for Ethan, and
the widows' group held a combination bridal shower and
"graduation party" for Barbara. One member gave a bridal
shower gift with a card inscribed, "Have fun on your senior
trip!"

John and I were special guests at the wedding, driving
the happy newlyweds from the church to the reception in
our Model A decorated with ribbons, streamers, a "Just Married" sign and a tail of trailing tin cans. When we got to the
village limits, Barbara asked if we'd take them around town
for a rootie-toot "like the kids do." As we went through town
blowing the *ah-ooga* horn and bull horn she said, "It's been so
long since I've laughed like this—let's go around again!"

Life Lessons Learned

Our experience with these support groups caused us to
change our lifestyle. We had organized daily life quite tradi-
tionally because our skills fell into those areas—I did cooking,
housework, secretarial work; John mowed the lawn, shoveled,
did home and car maintenance. But we soon saw the challenges that rigid traditional roles posed for widowed per-

sons—trying to manage finances without ever having written a check, driving a car without knowing how to put gas in it, needing to eat without knowing how to grocery shop or prepare simple meals. Along with the grief of losing a spouse these traditional roles presented major lifestyle changes or an identity crisis. So John and I decided we would share more tasks and learn from each other. He did some baking, cooking, cleaning, laundry; I learned how to check the car's oil level and tire pressure and pump gas (which came in handy when gas stations became self-serve only), and I acquired some basic business skills (like who to call for help). Once I even drove an 18-foot five-speed diesel truck sixty miles while John coached me (I already knew how to double-clutch!). Sharing new tasks was not only entertaining; it was useful when one of us was sick or away from home. Because our work frequently reminded us of how suddenly life can change, we learned to be flexible.

I continued to read and learn more about the grief process. Once I drove to a seminar in one of Michigan's cities to the south of us. I stayed overnight with friends and then had to drive for twenty minutes in rush hour traffic to get to the seminar location. My friend had given me a good map, showing which lanes to be in, what cross street would come just before I had to turn, and so forth. Even so, it was scary to be in a station wagon on a busy freeway sandwiched between two semis in morning rush hour traffic. (It was comforting to know the people from that area found the freeways scary, too.) At that seminar I expressed concern for people who lose a loved one and amazement that anyone gets through such loss. A wise and kindly nun told me, "When you have fully healed from your own grief, you will know." I learned that self care, particularly unpacking and sorting through my own grief baggage, was necessary for me before I could be of help to others.

At another grief support meeting I talked with one of John's mortuary school instructors, who was also working full time at a funeral home. He seemed a bit burned out. At one point he asked, "Why does John stay working at a small-town funeral home? I know he admires his dad and wanted to help, but he could have any job in the state. Why … ?"

" … Podunkville?" I ended his sentence for him.

"Well, yes."

"John loves his work and its variety so much that I can't get him out of town on a vacation. He's happy and fulfilled— even if we sometimes border on poverty!"

Some years later I read, in *Native Wisdom for White Minds* by Anne Wilson Schaef, that native people define "wealth" as living and working on the land of one's ancestors.[2] Viewed from that perspective, rather than by the accumulation of money and "stuff," our life is rich indeed.

As I continued reading and attending seminars I learned about grief experiences other than death—less visible losses such as burnout, loss of a job, loss of a pet, loss of a cherished idea, divorce, emotional abuse—and that, indeed, as my mother-in-law had once observed, these life events can be more difficult than the grief resulting from death. For example, when someone goes through a divorce, friends rarely bring casseroles or send cards and flowers. Divorce is not ritualized in our culture. For one of my seminary projects I researched and wrote a "removal of rings" ritual to be used by divorcing persons.

Since no two grief experiences are alike, it is helpful to have a variety of resources from which to choose. Abbey Press offers *CareNotes* on many topics.[3] Each note lists additional resources. *How To Survive the Loss of a Love* by Melba Colgrove and others is a small but helpful book, easy to read.[4]

Camping in the Family "Vehicle"

While we continued to read and attend ongoing learning events, we also took weekend or overnight trips. When John's folks were still able to take care of the business, we could visit relatives and friends out of town, go shopping, and attend movies. Having grown up on a dairy farm with a confining daily schedule, however, I wished for a real family vacation—at least a week long. Shortly after we bought our used Cadillac hearse (still "unused" by us), John's parents encouraged us to go. John consented—as long as vacation expenses didn't exceed $350. I began to plan.

Our converted station wagon was a multipurpose vehicle (with detachable side panels and curtains). We could camp in it, using a foam mattress in back for John and me and the bench-style front seat as a bed for Paul. I consulted seasoned campers for advice, then set about making sloppy joe mixture and chili and froze them in quart-size containers. When it was time to go, I packed the meals, along with frozen strawberries, hamburgers, hot dogs, bacon, and eggs, in a Styrofoam ice chest. A borrowed Coleman camp stove along with pots, pans, and canned goods slid easily under the seats. We stashed our clothing in the well beneath the back seats.

On the day of departure the wagon was packed and ready to go, but John was stalling. He couldn't find a jacket he wanted to take. Then he had to go to the corner gas station, get some mints, and say goodbye to friends. Exasperated that all the planning—and the entire trip—were being jeopardized by his dawdling, I demanded, "John, get in this car and *get us out of town before someone dies!*" Finally we made it out of the yard and into Ohio that Saturday night. Sunday night we camped at a farm-like campground in West Virginia before heading for the Blue Ridge Parkway. There was just one rule: no calling home until we arrived at our destination. We

made it to Crab Tree Meadows on the Blue Ridge Parkway that Monday night. Before we ate our supper of chicken
noodle soup, John called home and learned that someone had
died suddenly just minutes after we left town and the funeral
would be Tuesday. His dad teased, "Is it okay if I use *your hearse*
for the funeral tomorrow?"

John was quiet that night and the next day as we ate fast
food in Gatlinburg and drove northwest through Tennessee.
All of a sudden he tapped his watch and said, "Dad should
be getting those flowers over to the church right now!" I
replied, "Oh my! We got your body out of town—but not
your mind!"

We didn't attempt a long vacation together again until after John's dad died and Paul had graduated from college. That
time we flew to Arizona in January. Before we left, we filled
out forms with information for our own obituaries and death
certificates. This time we decided not to call home at all while
we were away. We visited relatives, enjoyed the mountains and
the warmth, went boating, went to the zoo and botanical gar-
dens. We returned to a cold welcome. Our car was completely
buried in snow at the airport, and there had been three funerals in our absence. The funeral director from the next town
had worked hard—assisted by my parents and others.

Gradually we learned it was easier for us to get off the yard
one at a time, so we began taking separate vacations. Whoever
was traveling called home each night, which allowed us the
best of two worlds, sharing travel experiences and home life.
The year Paul and Joy were married 400 miles away, John and
I traveled together on four separate weekends for their engagement party, showers, and wedding. Three out of the four
trips were cut short by deaths back home.

During our first decade in funeral service, I sometimes
envied people who worked nine-to-five, had fringe benefits,
paid vacations, and could actually plan their lives. We always

had to pay our own Social Security taxes and health insurance and the coverage wasn't as good as employer-paid benefits. Our work consumed us 24/7, taking priority over planned social events. We often drove separately to church and family gatherings in case John had a fire and rescue run or there was a death call.

On the other hand, while we lived in our rented homes, I enjoyed the garden, the babbling brook outside our bedroom window, neighborhood children trout fishing, solitude for reading and studying for Bible classes I taught, schlepping, not having to punch a clock or drive daily on winter roads, and having the school, grocery store, post office, and bank within easy walking distance.

But after ten years, John's dad became ill and needed a more private and quiet place. So, with help from the local fire department, we moved his folks into a rented ranch-style home and ourselves into the funeral home.

Clearing Clutter Versus Caring for Others

We had to hit the ground running. During the first week while I was still unpacking boxes, there were three funerals. I typed death certificates and made folders, while trying to hang curtains and keep the place organized and tidy with counters kept clear. But in spite of my best efforts, there were still curtain rods lying on the kitchen counter during the first visitation, and I was exhausted. The daughter of the man who had died watched me as I bustled. She knew my background, which stressed a neat-and-tidy environment. Sitting on a stool at our kitchen counter, she quietly liberated me. She said, "I think I'd feel more at home if there was a little more clutter." In the years that followed I may have learned that lesson too well, but if clutter makes people feel at home, I can do clutter! Actually, clutter happens naturally; mail comes in and before it's sorted the phone rings or someone stops by and we get sidetracked. I often remind myself of the lesson I learned that first week: People are more important than stuff.

With our move into the funeral home came a big change for me. I missed the big yard, the stream, garden, and trees, but most of all I missed the solitude. Our home had suddenly become a public place subject to callers at any time of day. One night around eleven the local police officer noticed our lights still on and stopped by for coffee after responding to a fight at the bar. While he was drinking coffee, one of the parties in the fight also saw our lights and the cruiser out front. He came walking into the house without knocking or ringing the doorbell. "Is this the police station?" he demanded.

The Old House Gets Updated

After living in the funeral home a short time we noticed its structural needs There was little insulation; the bedrooms were upstairs, which was not heated; the only bathroom was on the main floor; there was little closet space. If someone came to the house before I got up, I had two options: stay upstairs until they left, or walk past the entrance and through the dining room and living room to the bathroom in my nightgown. Whenever I was upstairs and needed my robe it was downstairs—and vice versa. And someone always came to the door when I was in the bathroom and John was gone. The only bathroom in the house had to be available during family conferences, visitations, and funerals. So began the first of many do-it-yourself remodeling projects: the upstairs, three stages in three years, which involved tearing out old horsehair plaster and lath, replacing the old chimney, insulating, rewiring, dry walling, painting, and putting in a much-needed second bathroom.

When the upstairs project was completed we started on the main floor, covering the chapel's dark walnut paneling with light-reflective wallpaper, smoothing and papering the walls in the dining room and living room, replacing windows, insulating, leveling floors, installing an accessible rest room, building a ramp to the entrance in front, living in the place all the while.

The bathroom project grew into a five-room project. My cousin helped John while I became the project "go-fer." One day I returned from an errand to discover that there was no floor in the bathroom area and the guys were pushing wheelbarrow loads of dirt through the front door and dumping them in "the pit" where the floor had been. When a rag fell down a vent pipe, my cousin used his ingenuity and a fishing line to get it out. On another day the three of us knelt together in the bathroom-to-be to design and create a template for a banjo-shaped countertop to accommodate the door opening. John built bathroom cabinets using wood from casket shipping trays.

When a new Federal ruling caused an increase in paperwork, we added filing cabinets in our dining room-office and used more cupboard space for office supplies.

The daily life in our mom-and-pop funeral home is similar to that of many in small towns throughout the country—before there were big conglomerates, before undertakers were called funeral directors and hearses were called coaches. To make a living, most small-town funeral directors had other jobs or enterprises. Some were florists, owned furniture stores, or had part-time jobs like John and his dad always did. "Undertakers" wore many hats for two reasons—to supplement income and to build community in the villages where they lived and served.

Buying a family business presented challenges economically and relationally, but with love and hard work it became mutually beneficial. We inherited a good name—which is "more desirable than great riches" (Proverbs 22:1). We benefited from John's parents' wisdom and insight, and their presence provided flexibility in our schedule. They, in turn, had free housing so they could enjoy their retirement years in spite of having no retirement savings. Their legacy was a life of service, trusting the wisdom: "Give, and it will be given to you." (Luke 6:38) Through all the ups and downs in income they were never hungry, had everything they needed, and never ran out of money.

Since moving into the funeral home I've learned much. While some people go through life setting goals and moving step-by-step toward them, this approach has not always worked for me. When the things I had hoped and planned for didn't happen, I gradually learned to trust a Higher Wisdom, exchanging my plans, hopes, and dreams for the challenges and opportunities that were put in my path.

Perhaps the most difficult transition for me was moving from a private home to a semi-public place, combining home and business under one roof. While faith, like yeast in bread-making, may be incubated in solitude, it must eventually be mixed, kneaded, and allowed to rise so that it can be baked to completion—a pattern much like the Covenant of Ur in the table on the next page.

Covenant	Genesis 12:1–3	Breadmaking	My Life Stages
Promise	I will bless you	Incubation	Solitude
Purpose	That you may be a blessing	Mixing/ Kneading	Struggling/ Integrating
Prophecy	Through you the world is blessed	Rising/ Baking/ Sharing	Peace/Unity Integrating

Afterthoughts

1. How do you see a pattern of growth in your life?

Three

WHAT DO THE CHILDREN (AND PETS) SAY?

"Out of the mouths of babes and infants ... "
Psalm 8:2, NRSV

*"I tell you the truth, unless you change and become like children,
you will never enter the kingdom of heaven."*
Matthew 18:3

"Peek-a-boo!" This timeless game is one of a child's earliest experiences of presence, separation, and reunion. It becomes a favorite pastime soon after their incubation, passage, and birth. This simple game also resonates with adults who have experienced many daily cycles of activity, sleep, and awakening—or times of togetherness, separation, and reunion. Peek-a-boo may symbolize nature's cycle of daylight, darkness, and sunrise—and is not unlike the grief process, which moves from orientation through disorientation, and eventually to reorientation. It may be like the journey of faith—life, death, and resurrection. Peek-a-boo ritualizes the rhythm of life's ongoing cycle and offers assurance that new beginnings always await.

In the cycle of life, the very young and the very old are next to one another and seem most naturally in touch with this inner wisdom. Grandma Nelda had had a stroke just before her youngest great-grandson was born. She never regained her ability to speak, yet there was a magical connection between Grandma Nelda and baby Kevin. The moment they made eye contact both burst into laughter as if each intuitively knew what the other was thinking or "saying." Language ability was neither key nor barrier to their relationship. This is often obvious when babies or children visit nursing homes.

The presence of children at visitations and funerals helps balance the pain of loss, separation, and grief. Children, by their very presence, bring new life into the midst of sadness and loss. They are living reminders of life's ongoing cycle. Even though they may not fully realize the significance of a visitation or funeral at the time, children do remember these times as important family events in which they were included. Life in the parlors has given us an opportunity to see firsthand the many ways children reaffirm life and faith.

Some children stick close to their parents when they first come to the funeral home. Others seem at home and initiate conversation. When 5-year-old Amy's teacher came to the visitation for Amy's grandpa, Amy said, "Grandpa was sick. He's dead now. Wanna come and see?" Taking her teacher by the hand Amy led her to the casket and said, "You can touch him. He feels cold." After her teacher had come, talked, seen, and touched, Amy went back to play with the other children—and the toys.

Busy Hands Heal Young Hearts

We have a toy box and other non-electronic activities such as viewing disks, jigsaw puzzles, brain teasers, and books in the living room. We also have molding clay, paper, pencils, crayons, and other art materials. A family member usually supervises the children while the visitation takes place "in the next room"—a metaphor for death. In this way children can be near their parents and also participate in the visitation at their own level, processing their feelings while their hands are busy.

I learned the "hospitality of the toy box" from "Aunt Mettie," honorary aunt of everyone in the village. Although she had no children, Aunt Mettie often invited families with children of similar ages to her home on Sunday evenings. She had a toy box filled with unusual toys. She provided games, puzzles, and snacks for children and young people to enjoy while the adults visited.

Food for the Body, Sustenance for the Soul

Speaking of snacks, I keep juice boxes on hand for children and offer them upon their parents' permission. Juice can also be helpful for diabetics or those who experience low blood sugar due to shock or irregular eating patterns. Nutritional support is vital to the grieving of all ages, and I've learned that certain kinds of foods are more beneficial than others. The addition of healthy snacks between meals may be helpful. It may also be beneficial to eat less but eat more frequently. Taking vitamins and other nutrition supplements may also be helpful. While some "comfort food" is okay, it's generally best to avoid junk foods—those with highly processed flour and sugar. Whole grains, honey, maple syrup, and other natural foods are more nutritious. Organic foods contain more nutrients than foods that have been grown with herbicides, pesticides, and artificial fertilizers.

Many families have visitation from two to four in the afternoon, have dinner together, and then return for visitation from seven to nine. One afternoon a family brought children between the ages of four and eight to the visitation of their great-grandfather. The children moved rather quickly from the chapel to the toy box in the living room. They played well together and displayed big imaginations. Using small plastic bricks, they built elaborate farmyards, moving animals about with trucks and trains. At four o'clock, they reluctantly left for the dinner hour. When dinner was barely finished they begged their parents, "Can we go back to the *funeral home?*"

We're honored when children enjoy being at the funeral home, but we had no idea how much the little ones thought of our place until 3-year-old Ashley came to view her grandpa. Her daddy picked her up in his arms and held her so she could see Grandpa, explaining, "Grandpa has gone to heaven." Whereupon Ashley said, "Then this must be heaven!"

Not all children size up the situation as quickly as Ashley. They may watch, listen, and ask many questions before making their own assessments. Four-year-old Nicole was at the visitation for her great uncle, who had died suddenly at the age of fifty-two. She wondered why he was "sleeping" and kept checking the casket to see if he "woke up yet." She peppered her family with questions and looked in the other rooms, gathering information. After a while she took pencil and paper and began drawing. When she finished, she interpreted: "Dis is a bird ... dis is a butterfly ... and dis is Uncle-Bobby-in-a-box."

Sometimes children test out explanations they've been given and show us new meaning. Seven-year-old Trevor watched carefully as we got the church ready for his great-grandmother's funeral. As we were placing floral arrangements, he came to the front of the church and said, "You're going to lay her up here (on the altar), aren't you?"

John said, "We'll move the altar and put her casket in that place."

Trevor continued: "Then you're going to take her to the cemetery and put her in a *safe*, right?" *Safe … Vault.*

"Yes, Trevor, after the funeral we're going to put Grandma in a *safe* in the cemetery."

When death comes suddenly and unexpectedly, parents may be too shocked to give careful attention to children's needs. Still, children wonder, ask questions, and learn. Four-year-old Robin and five-year-old Rudy were fascinated by the hearse, the funeral procession, and committal. They wanted to stay at the cemetery, watch the entire burial, and ride back to the church in the hearse. Their exhausted parents consented and left them with John. On the way back to the church for the luncheon they peppered John with questions. They were naturally curious and unafraid.

Sometimes children have surprising reactions when told that someone they know has died. Three-year-old Curtis lived near Uncle Mike and Aunt Carrie. One day Uncle Mike, who had been ill, died at home. When Curtis learned from his mother that Uncle Mike had died, he probed, "Where is Uncle Mike?"

Mom said, "He went to heaven."

Curtis predicted, "Aunt Carrie is going to be mad!"

When third-grader Adam died following an accident, most adults in the village were shocked and heartbroken. Counselors visited the school to assist teachers and be available for students. On the day of the visitation, teachers, still deep in grief, came to the funeral home on their lunch hour to prepare themselves before bringing the children to the visitation. But when the children arrived, there were few tears. They were mostly curious. They wanted to see his shoes, so John opened the foot panel of the little casket to show them. Some had drawn pictures and written letters, which they placed in the casket. When their questions were answered, they were ready to go back to school. Throughout their remaining years in school, this class formed unusually deep bonds. There were not the divisions and rivalries seen in other classes. While they seemed nonchalant, it appeared much maturation and transformation were taking place as they wove this early experience of loss into their lives.

As I watch children at the funeral home I can still recall my first experiences with death. When I was in the fifth grade, a classmate and friend died suddenly, but I wasn't able to attend her visitation or funeral because I had strep throat. When I recovered, I didn't want to go back to school. And when I went back I didn't want to play. For a while I hung out with troublemakers.

My first experience with a family visitation and funeral was when my great uncle was killed beneath a car when the jack slipped. I remember the strange mixture of shock, sadness, and curiosity—wanting to touch, yet feeling repulsed by the coldness and unresponsiveness of his skin. I remember all the adults seeming sad and reserved. I remember crying in the car on the way to the cemetery. I remember the entire experience as devoid of any laughter or joy.

During my freshman year of high school a classmate was killed in a car accident. We attended his funeral as a class. This, too, was a sad and joyless time.

Then my grandpa died of a heart attack in a doctor's office. I remember how cold and stony his arm felt when I touched him. I remember my mom and other relatives crying. And I remember feeling deeply sad and sobbing throughout the funeral.

I continued to feel sad whenever anyone I knew died, especially accidents that claimed the lives of young people in our community. Now, as I observe children in our funeral home playing, asking questions, even greeting other visitors, I wish my early experiences with death and grief could have been more like theirs. It is, however, heartwarming to be able to provide children with a warm, home-like, child-friendly setting so that they can experience death as a natural part of life.

The Undertaker's Son

If my childhood grief experiences had been more like those of children today, I might have been better prepared to field Paul's questions during John's apprenticeship and mortuary school years. As it was, I was grateful when John was available to answer Paul's questions since he didn't seem to carry as much "grief baggage" as I did. I remember one day the three of us were together in a station wagon transporting a body three hours' distance. The body was in a black zippered pouch, which John had moved to one side so 3-year-old Paul could have room to play—these were the days before we knew children should always be belted into their seats. I had bought a new plastic truck for Paul, and he climbed in back to play while John and I talked. After a while Paul interrupted, "Hey Dad, there's a dead body back here!"

John said, "There is?" And Paul went on playing.

But many times John wasn't there because he was working and taking classes. One time, at the funeral home where he worked, there was a service for a toddler who had died in his sleep. He was placed in a small casket wearing a striped polo shirt, clasping his teddy bear and truck. This really tugged at our heartstrings since Paul was the same age. Although we talked softly out of his earshot, Paul seemed to have sensed the situation. Later that evening while John was at work and I was sewing in our bedroom, Paul climbed onto our bed, crawled under the comforter and tucked the edge under his chin. He carefully positioned one hand over the other, closed his eyes and without a smile, barely breathing, said, "I'm dead." I looked at him, horrified at how "really dead" he looked and how awful that would be—wishing John were there, glad Paul's eyes were closed. Knowing Paul's attitude toward death was being formed by my reaction, I managed to say, "It certainly looks that way," and continued going through the motions of sewing.

Regardless of any explanations I gave him about death, Paul had his own. When he was three, I took him to a great aunt's funeral. He asked why she was "sleeping."

I said, "She's dead."

He said, "No she's not dead. I know dat lady. She will get up and go to her house."

At the funeral home where John worked, there wasn't always time for a dinner break, so Paul and I would meet him in the garage and "picnic" among the floral deliveries—with the added attraction of a soda pop machine. After one such picnic we went inside the home and Paul saw a uniformed police officer in a casket. He said, "I want to see dat man." We went with him to the casket. He said, "Where's his legs?" John raised the foot panel and showed him. Paul made no comment until he and I were on our way home. He was quiet for a while, then he said, "Dat was a nice man."

I said, "Yes, he was a nice man."

"Dat's not fair."

"What's not fair?"

"He was a nice man and he died."

"No, that's not fair."

During the year of mortuary school, John's anatomy and physiology charts hung in our hallway. Sometimes Paul asked questions about the musculoskeletal or circulatory systems. I held him up and explained how the heart pumps blood all over the body through the arteries (drawn in red) and returns it through the veins (drawn in blue). I figured he probably wouldn't understand or retain the information. A year later he came home from Sunday School, upset about a song they had sung. I asked, "What was the song?" With hands on hips he said indignantly, "They sang, 'Into my heart, come into my heart, Lord Jesus.' *Don't they know if you had Jesus in your heart you'd be dead?*"

When we first took over the family business, we installed an off-premise extension phone in our home. We taught Paul how to politely answer the funeral phone and ask "May I tell who's calling?" before turning over the phone to us. One evening while we were having dinner, the funeral phone rang and Paul ran to practice his new skill. But, after asking who was calling, he looked perplexed. Without putting his hands over the receiver he said, "Dad, it's for you. I don't know who it is, but I think he's drunk!" The caller turned out to be the United Methodist minister.

Since Paul often visited Grandad and Grandma at the funeral home, it didn't occur to us that he felt stigmatized by the profession, but from time to time there were clues. At junior high church camp when counselors asked their parents' occupations, Paul offered: "My Dad's an undertaker; our motto is 'you stab 'em, we slab 'em.'" That drew wild laughter from the kids. Two years later when we camped there as a family, a counselor still remembered the incident.

When we moved into the funeral home, with its more public nature, Paul was in high school. He began developing his funeral-director's-kid role into an attention-getting art of sorts. He wrote a descriptive theme entitled "The Messy Prep Room" designed to gross out his teacher, a woman. In another class he gave a graphic speech about hitting road kill with his motorcycle. Same purpose.

We dismissed this as kid stuff, but at a funeral directors' family picnic the children talked among themselves and seemed surprised to learn that other kids also had to be quiet when the phone rang or walk and talk softly if they lived above the funeral home. The parents were also surprised to learn that their children had felt "weird." I remember the day Paul had an *aha!* moment about his role. He announced: "We're not *weird*; we're *eccentric!*"

As much as his dad and grandad would have loved to pass the small-town funeral home to the third generation, they realized this is a vocation that needs to be chosen from the heart. Paul's passions were motorcycling and snowmobiling. He chose to work on farms and in a factory rather than at the funeral home to finance his hobbies. He learned much about mechanics while repairing and maintaining his motorcycle and snowmobile. His favorite movies were *Star Wars* and *Star Trek*, and cartoons *The Far Side* and *Calvin and Hobbes*, favorites of many engineers (and I confess to feeling a kinship with Calvin's parents). It's not surprising, then, that he chose engineering rather than funeral service as a profession.

A Long Line of Funeral Home Felines

Because Paul was an only child, we adopted feline family members, but only one at a time. Ms. Kitty, a long-haired tabby-and-white, was Paul's Christmas-present kitten when he was in second grade. We had lost his first cat, Katrina, to feline leukemia and waited three months before getting another. Ms. Kitty's kittenish surprises and games brought laughter and delight to our home once again. She played "baseball" by batting a paper wad from her superior position atop the refrigerator, and she "spoke" in long sentences with expressive voice inflection. Ms. Kitty was eight years old when we moved into the funeral home, so she was our first funeral home cat. She set up an all-town command station inside the front door and became an official greeter. For the rare people with allergies or aversions to cats, we secluded Ms. Kitty.

In Ms. Kitty's senior years she avoided young children. But she would make exceptions. When 7-year-old Christy, who had traveled from Arizona to attend her grandpa's funeral, became inconsolably weepy after the service, we let her cry for a while. Then I held Ms. Kitty over my shoulder and knelt to let Christy pet her. Ms. Kitty calmly purred Christy's sobs into giggles as Christy was reminded of her own kitty back home.

Each night after a visitation we turn off the lights and close the doors to the chapel. One morning, however, after a visitation for an elderly farmer, we found Ms. Kitty sleeping on the sofa in the chapel. She had eluded us and taken the night watch. At the funeral that day, the grandchildren told stories of Grandma insisting, "The cats belong in the barn." But they told how Grandpa would sneak cats into the house for them to play with and how much they had enjoyed the kitties. We still wonder why Ms. Kitty chose this particular time to remain in the chapel overnight.

During Ms. Kitty's twentieth summer, John and I were gone on four different weekends for Paul and Joy's engagement party, showers, and wedding. Ms. Kitty was pampered by a friend through these times. But one week after the wedding, Ms. Kitty refused all food and spent most of her time outside communing with nature and looking beyond. It was as if she were saying, "I raised your kid, but now he has a wife so I'm out of here." Two weeks later I found her in the basement, lame and crying when she saw me. I said, "Ms. Kitty, you're not going to die down here by yourself," wrapped her in a flannel blanket, took her upstairs, and rocked her. Even though she was deaf, I told her how much we loved her and thanked her for all the laughter and comfort she had given. She purred and "talked" back as if thanking us. That evening, while John was away, Ms. Kitty died, still purring, in my arms.

The next morning I wrote a eulogy that included the Noahic covenant: "I am establishing my covenant with you and your descendants after you, *and with every living creature that is with you, the birds, the domestic animals, and every animal of the earth …* " (Genesis 9:9–10, NRSV, italics mine). I laminated the eulogy along with photos and placed them in the box with Ms. Kitty. John buried her under our living room window, which faces east. Later that day it began raining while the sun was shining. Looking eastward over her grave we saw a huge double rainbow, sign of the Noahic covenant. It was as if Ms. Kitty were saying, "I'm not down there; I'm up here in a beautiful and happy place."

There was a calico kitten I'd been eyeing but wouldn't bring home because I didn't want to crush Ms. Kitty's spirit. From her new perch Ms. Kitty seemed to be saying, "I want you to be happy, too. Your place could use some animation, so go ahead and get the kitten. Name her 'Rainbow' to remind everyone that animals are included in the covenant." Soon thereafter our vet sent a copy of "The Rainbow Bridge," a poem about pets waiting to escort those who have loved them across a rainbow bridge to a bright and happy place.

Because Rainbow needed a home, we adopted her a few days later. We were still grieving Ms. Kitty, of course, so Rainbow had some big paws to fill. But she charmed us as her predecessor had; made us laugh and helped move our lives forward again. She had apparently fed herself with foraged table scraps and was a living demonstration of joy and thanksgiving as she "captured" a frozen pea and turned it into a delightful dance. Rainbow also proved adept at helping herself to any "people food" left on the counters at night. She charmed visitors and earned the distinction of "the kitty with the curly tail." Many visitors took pictures of her as well as of each other at visitations.

When John's mom came to visit, she and Rainbow developed a breakfast ritual, Rainbow on one barstool, Grandma on the other. Grandma would hand a Cheerio to Rainbow. If it was soaked in milk Rainbow ate it out of Grandma's hand. If not, it became a toy. Whenever Grandma visited, even while on vacation from the nursing home, they carried on this breakfast ritual. Sadly, however, after only four years as a family member, Rainbow was hit by a car and crossed the "rainbow bridge" two months before Grandma.

After Rainbow, we hadn't planned on having a cat for awhile, but a few months later sleek-and-sable Lucy (with a Siamese heritage) came into our lives because she, too, needed a home. While she was adapting to life in the parlors, we had a service for Nick, an elderly fellow who had faithfully fed feral cats for many years. Friends and family requested that Lucy be allowed to "attend" the service. When Lucy heard me speaking at the service, she came into the chapel, approached each person, then wandered out.

Later a Native American speaker said, "We believe that after the soul leaves the body it is free to go where it wants. One man became a robin because all he ever wanted to do was sit in a tree, sing to people, and make them happy." She continued, "You can believe what you want, but when Lucy walked into the room and greeted everyone, she did so exactly the way Nick entered a room and greeted people."

Regarding the relationship between people and animals, an elderly farmer observed, "You can tell a lot about someone's character by the way they treat animals. Some people go to church but mistreat animals. Their beliefs are unattractive to me."

All Creatures Great and Small

Animal wisdom has been helpful to me when I visit people
in their homes. I went to visit Hazel, a farmer's wife who was
dying. Her family cautioned that she might not welcome my
visit. Her daughter Beth and golden retriever Sunny met me
at the door. After I passed Sunny's initial sniff test, Skeets, a
tiny but lively kitten adopted from the barn, "attacked" Sunny,
and the two put on quite a show. Good-natured Sunny allowed Skeets to attack repeatedly even though she could have
ended the assaults quickly with one downward stroke of her
paw. We watched together until the performers tired. Because
I had passed the "animal test," Hazel let me stay. Since Hazel
had served many farmers' breakfasts through the years, I asked
her if I could read a story about Jesus cooking breakfast for
the disciples on the beach. She nodded. I read John 21:4–14.
Then I asked her if I could "serve breakfast" to her. Again she
nodded. As I was breaking the bread, Sunny got up, walked
to my side, and stood reverently anticipating her portion. I
served her first. From then on there was no question of my
welcome in Hazel's home—and news soon spread through
the village that I gave communion to dogs.

While serving as an interim pastor, I was asked to visit
Bernadine, an elderly shut-in who had a variety of health
problems, self-pity among them. She had recently lost her
beloved canary and had gotten a new one. She told me at
length how much she missed the old one and why the new
one didn't please her as much as the old one. In fact, the new
one would no longer sing for her. He sat at the bottom of his
cage with his back toward us.

I asked his name, went to the cage, and said, "Hi Harry, I'm
Celia, and I'm pleased to meet you. Do you think we could
be friends?" Harry made no response. I turned my attention

back to Bernadine. "I have a story I'd like to tell you." For the next fifteen minutes I sat on the floor, pulling materials out of a box, telling a story of God's love for all, both people and animals. Bernadine and I focused on the story, and when it was finished, we looked up to see Harry, neck stretched over the edge of the cage, watching and listening.

Some time after Bernadine and Harry found God's love together, 7-year-old neighbor Matt came to our door with a just-hatched bird that had fallen to the ground and died. I knew that Matt had lost his aunt, uncle, and grandma within a year's time. So, I found a small jewelry box and got some lint from the dryer. Matt nested the baby bird in the softly cushioned "casket." I asked him to name the bird. He named it "Tommy." We thanked God for Tommy's all-too-brief life on earth, blessed him, and committed his tiny body to the earth and his spirit to God who gave it. We dug a grave. Matt put the box inside, wrote Tommy's name on a stone, and placed it over the grave as a monument. Nature and ritual helped us to rediscover our own capacity for compassion, hope, and healing.

Nature offers many resources for hope. When an elderly friend had "locked-in syndrome" and was unable to move any part of her body, other than her eyes and lower jaw, following a stroke, I asked a young artist to draw a picture of a caterpillar, cocoon, and butterfly. I showed the picture to my friend, talking about the familiar life the caterpillar represented, the cocoon stage she was experiencing, and the glorious life that awaited her. She moved her eyes up and down to indicate she had heard and understood.

Some families use nature's symbolism in creative ways. At the funeral of a teenager who had been wheelchair bound for many years, family members released doves who instinctively "flew home," leaving everyone to wonder about their own "homing instinct."

Psalm 23, the Scripture most often chosen for funerals, is also nature-rich. It speaks of green pastures, shadowy valleys, and the tender relationship between shepherd and sheep. It is the story of a shepherd's annual cycle—and our life's cycle.

Families often choose hymns which speak of nature. "In the Garden," "How Great Thou Art," "Rock of Ages," "His Eye Is on the Sparrow," and "Savior, Like a Shepherd Lead Us" all speak of God in nature and make God's love and care more tangible in the midst of life's uncertainty and loss.

Out of the mouths of babes, children, animals, and nature come wisdom and hope to balance times of loss and sadness. Children, animals, and nature remind us of life's ongoing cycle, bring heaven's joy to the earth, and invite all to sing of peace on earth as angels and shepherds did long ago.

(*See Appendix I for children's materials.*)

Afterthoughts

1. What were some of your early childhood experiences with loss and grief?

2. How do you see these experiences now?

Four

WHY FUSS OVER THE BODY?

She poured perfume on my body beforehand to prepare for my burial …
wherever the gospel is preached throughout the world,
what she has done will also be told, in memory of her.

Mark 14:8–9

They sat around our table: Addie, a frail, elderly woman whose husband Sam had just died, her daughter Rebecca, and her son Vince. Addie said little. Sad and exhausted, she sat between Rebecca and Vince, who answered all questions and made all decisions.

After providing the information needed for the death certificate and obituary, Vince and Rebecca said they wanted a direct cremation. No viewing. No service. No fuss. Addie protested meekly. Rebecca asserted, "Remember, Mom, this is what we talked about earlier. This is the best way."

John asked Addie, "Would you like to see Sam?" She brightened. Vince said, "That won't be necessary. We'll just remember him the way he was." Addie found her voice. "Yes, I'd like to see him."

And so with Vince on one side and Rebecca on the other, Addie walked into the chapel and gazed lovingly at Sam lying on a cot. Vince and Rebecca allowed Addie a brief moment, then pulled her away and walked her out of the chapel and out the door. Addie looked back longingly as she was hustled forever away from the body of her husband, the man she loved, ate with, talked with, and slept with for fifty-six years.

This scenario is becoming more and more common as some family members want a no-fuss "disposal," while others need time with the body to actualize and process the loss. Ironically, many of those opting for quick disposal could easily afford a full-service funeral, while families of lesser means are willing to sacrifice to have a visitation, funeral, burial, and monument.

Funerals Heal the Living

Families may choose the services they wish based on tradition, religious beliefs, circumstances of death, economy, or instructions their loved one has given. Sometimes individuals state their wishes without discussing them with the family or considering the long-range consequences.

"When I go, don't fuss. Just cremate me," Henry Fulton always told his family. But when he died his wife Betty was torn between his expressed wishes and their faith tradition, which involved viewing, a funeral service at the church, a shared meal, and burial in the church cemetery. John told Betty it was possible to have a service with the body present and then cremate. However, there was time pressure since state laws required "disposition" within forty-eight hours if not embalmed. Since most of the Fultons' seven children lived some distance away and were en route (before cell phones were in common use), Betty had to make the decision alone. She decided on a direct cremation without a service.

One by one the Fulton children and their families arrived, expecting a traditional funeral service. And one by one they expressed anger toward Betty for robbing them of a viewing, funeral, and the community support they were anticipating. Didn't she know Dad wasn't serious? He just didn't want to talk about death and dying.

At the funeral home we received many phone calls from members of the church and community asking about service arrangements and friends who were preparing to send flowers, make a kettle of soup or a batch of muffins, attend the viewing and service, or help with the church dinner. When we said there wasn't going to be a viewing or service, there was stunned silence on the other end of the line, followed by disbelief, then, "What can we do?" and a perplexed "Goodbye." The community's usual way of offering love and support to a bereaved family was disrupted.

In the months that followed, Betty and her children called the funeral home frequently—as if searching for something they couldn't quite find. Friends noticed the family's difficulty in moving on. They weren't surprised, several years later, when Betty died in another state and the children had her body flown to their hometown for a visitation, church funeral, dinner, and burial, which they all agreed they needed. In the presence of the church and community, they told everyone they found the comfort, support, and peace they had long needed.

The Fulton family's struggle between their father's expressed wishes and the family's faith tradition is occurring with greater frequency. Everyone's needs could have been met with forethought and mutual consideration. At the time of death the body becomes the legal "property" of the next-of-kin. After a funeral home has been chosen, one of the most important decisions that survivors (or independent personal representatives) must make is what will be done with the body. If a visitation and funeral service with the body present are chosen, embalming is always advised by the funeral home—and required by state law if final disposition does not take place within forty-eight hours. The "methods of disposition" listed on the death certificate are burial, cremation, entombment, donation, storage, or removal (as to another facility or another state). (*See Appendix D for further details regarding methods of disposition.*)

If family members have discussed funeral arrangements in advance and made mutual decisions, everyone's struggle is eased during a difficult time. If family members are not in agreement regarding the arrangements, some funeral directors may facilitate family conferences, help the family reach consensus, or accommodate as many needs as possible. Funeral directors may ask that the family meet elsewhere, make decisions, and have the family member with "contractual authority" return to the funeral home with clear instructions. If family discussion doesn't take place until the time death occurs, it may be complicated by exhaustion, shock, distance, and time pressure.

Some reasons to choose direct cremation may be convenience, efficiency, and economy, especially in urban areas where funeral costs may be higher and burial space costly and scarce. There may also be historical, natural, biblical, health, cultural, social, and philosophical reasons for "due process" with the body.

The Human History of Death Rites

From earliest times people have held rites of various kinds to honor and remember the dead, appease the gods, or supply the dead with materials they may need for life in another world. The Egyptians embalmed so well that bodies are preserved to this day. They also built elaborate pyramids and

furnished them so that the soul would have worldly com
forts when it came to visit the dead. The Romans are cred-
ited with originating the rites of wearing black, walking in
procession, and raising mounds over the grave—customs that
were introduced in England when the Romans invaded in
43 C.E. Some African tribes slaughtered the deceased's family
and cattle to serve the dead. Australian tribes cut their own
bodies during ceremonies. Other customs included walking
backward or turning clothes inside out. Some native tribes
buried their dead in shallow graves to give back to nature—to
become food for animals. Others heaped rocks over bodies
to *prevent* them from becoming food for animals. The Vikings
placed their dead on boats, which were set on fire and pushed
out to sea.

In India, people build pyres to burn the dead, and the ash-
es are thrown into the sacred Ganges River. In the war torn
Middle East, some risk their lives to give a "proper burial."

In certain Native American cultures, when the chief dies,
the tribe gathers in the long house for rituals and storytelling.
This may go on for days or weeks. When there are no stories
left to tell it's time to elect a new chief. Many cultures hold
rituals involving the body in which friends of the deceased
build pyres, dig graves, or put the body in a canoe and send it
over a waterfall.

Historian Oliver McRae describes the increasing distance
at which deceased bodies are kept. At first there were wilder-
ness burials marked by stones. Then cemeteries were located
close to churches. Eventually cemeteries were located outside
city limits, bringing more detachment, greater psychological
distance, and funeral processions. Then came garden cemeteries with works of art providing beauty, reassurance of eternity,
elaborate ceremonies, sculpted angels. Central Park began as a
cemetery and was visited by 30,000 people a year. After two

world wars, the second of which brought mass incineration by the atomic bomb, memorial art became abstract. Spiritually reassuring angels were replaced by unadorned granite slabs. Funerals became short and somber "memorial services." Economy and efficiency now brought a vast empty lawn and small plaques lying flat on grass—resulting in social alienation—where we find ourselves today. And with the increase in cremations, funeral service has become "furnace service."[1]

In the natural world, when old trees die, they become "food" and "wisdom" for the younger trees. But with the practice of clearcutting forests there is no "body of wisdom" from which new trees can draw for growth.

In biblical culture, the ultimate honor was to be buried with one's ancestors, and the ultimate dishonor was nonburial. Patriarch Jacob's last request was to have his body entombed with his ancestors. When he died he was embalmed (Genesis 50:2), and his family made the trip from Egypt to Israel to honor his wishes (Genesis 47:29–31, 49:29–50:14). Joseph, the despised "dreamer" brother who ended up as royalty in Egypt and saved his family and others from famine, requested that his own bones be taken back to Israel and buried there when the nation returned. He was embalmed Egyptian style, and 400 years later Moses and Joshua honored his request (Genesis 50:24–26, Exodus 13:19, Joshua 24:32). Prophecy, oaths and covenants, and promise keeping were woven with proper burial, connecting generations in faith.

In the chronicles of Kings, there was a brief description of the king's accomplishments whether good or bad, and the account ended with the mode of burial. Kings who were good or not-totally-evil were buried with "their fathers" or with other royalty. An official time of national mourning was declared, often thirty days. If kings were judged evil, they were not buried with their more noble ancestors or royalty. Ahab and Jezebel were considered evil-to-the-max, killing prophets and other innocent people. Jezebel was thrown from a window and trampled by horses, her bones eaten by dogs. She received no burial at all—the ultimate dishonor (II Kings 9:10, 30–37). Her husband Ahab was to have met the same fate, but because he humbled himself he received a burial, although dogs licked his blood as it was washed from the chariot (I Kings 21:17–28, 22:29–38).

Honorable burial continued to be important in the ancient Hebrew tradition. The body was prepared with costly oil, and those (such as Joseph of Arimathea) who gave the honorable burial were especially blessed. The women closest to Jesus, who remained at his execution, headed for the tomb as soon as tradition permitted so that they could properly prepare Jesus's body. Those who did so were the first recipients of resurrection joy—the first proclaimers of the resurrection and a gospel of new beginnings. As they looked backward they could see that Jesus had prepared them for this task little by little. Jesus had raised a widow's son (as Elijah had done), and the raising of Lazarus showed Jesus's power over death. Jesus had promised to prepare a place for them (John 14:1–6), but this only made sense in retrospect. Most biblical accounts of death involved due process with the body, time to mourn, and provision for an afterlife.

Unprocessed Grief Takes Its Toll

Many healthcare professionals see the value of due process with the body. Counselors say many illnesses have their roots in unprocessed or incompletely processed grief experiences. Women who miscarry or abort a fetus often experience severe depression or other serious health problems years later.

When counselors help someone through an unprocessed grief experience, they use eye movement therapy, body movement, guided imagery, journaling, drawing, and so forth. All of these exercises are designed to make an abstract experience more concrete by using the senses—the body-mind-spirit connection—to process the loss, which is what viewing and funeral rituals are designed to do.

Recognizing the body-mind-spirit connection, nurses in hospitals, nursing homes, and hospices often concretely involve family members in the dying process. They offer support and nurture families throughout and then help them make the transition to a funeral home. Nurses and staff members often come to the visitation, wake, funeral, or memorial service, realizing that viewing the body is a concrete experience that can help survivors "actualize" the death of a loved one.

Genealogical societies recognize the need for actualizing and the need to connect with one's roots. Since the television miniseries *Roots* was first shown, more and more people stop at funeral homes, search vital records, and visit cemeteries where their ancestors were buried. In a mobile society, many people want and need a concrete experience that connects them with their ancestors.

Our mobile culture has other rituals—with the honorees' present—to mark the important events of life, such as birth, baptism, induction into organizations, graduation, birthdays, and marriages. Why would so many in this same culture choose to have the honored one absent in the rituals of death?

There are some cultural clues that the trend toward convenient and economical "disposal" without viewing or ritual may not be in keeping with our own inner values. When prominent public people, such as President John F. Kennedy, the Rev. Dr. Martin Luther King, Princess Diana, and Mother Theresa died; when the Murrah Building in Oklahoma City was bombed; when the World Trade Center's twin towers fell; when the Pentagon was attacked, when the space shuttles and their crews were lost; when military personnel, fire, and police officers died in the line of duty; or whenever there was an airline or other disaster, recovery of the bodies and rituals of remembrance became a central focus. The media responded to the national and international need to feel connected during times of tragedy and loss.

Filmmakers, likewise, understand the human need to make loss experiences concrete. To make death "real" on the screen they use caskets, churches, rituals, hearses, processions, people in dark clothing and sunglasses, open graves, and cemetery monuments.

Thomas Lynch, essayist, poet, and funeral director suggests one reason for the cultural shift may be Jessica Mitford's book, *The American Way of Death*, which lampooned the death care industry. Lynch points out that when Mitford experienced the loss of her parents and spouse she opted for quick "disappearing." Was her literary work, Lynch wondered, while entertaining, the product of her own unprocessed grief and anger displaced onto the death care profession?[2]

Is it possible that direct disposition without viewing, remembering together, and reweaving family and community may have detrimental long-range consequences? Will the money "saved" at the funeral home be exceeded by the costs of health care or counseling services? What is the cost to society when those with unresolved grief "act out" in violent ways? Does disconnecting from the body too quickly contribute to social alienation and violence?

In a culture of fast cars, fast food, instant communication, and instant gratification, grief still takes time. In a youth-oriented, death-denying, addictive, and violent culture in which viewing the body is seen as "barbaric," taking time to view the body can, like an old growth forest, yield accumulated wisdom needed for survival and growth. Rituals of remembrance and celebration offer words and symbols to process loss and deepen compassion. In his novel *The Five People You Meet In Heaven,* Mitch Albom's character, the Blue Man, wonders why people gather when others die and why they feel they should. He gives his own answer, "It is because the human spirit knows, deep down, that all lives intersect. That death doesn't just take someone, it misses someone else, and in the small distance between being taken and being missed, lives are changed."[3]

If people don't take time to remember together, what happens to family, community, nation, and culture? Do they lose their history? Warmth? Integrity? Depth? Peace? Joy? Unity? Connection to the earth? Humanity? Sense of community?

In the Twenty-third Psalm, the Good Shepherd prepares a table "in the presence of my enemies." Jesus prepared a table in the presence of the one who was about to betray him. In fact, he made the betrayer the guest of honor when initiating Holy Communion. This love of the enemy gave power and authenticity to the Eucharist, giving thanks in all things. The victorious nature of a Christian funeral asserts resurrection power *in the very presence* of death.

Gladstone may have been wondering about these things when he wrote: "Show me the way a nation cares for its dead, and I will measure for you with mathematical exactness the tender mercies of its people, their respect for the laws of their land, and their loyalty to high ideals."[4]

Afterthoughts

1. What benefits might there be from the viewing of the body or a funeral service with the body present? Or is viewing just a marketing ploy of the funeral industry?

2. How does the way we care for the dead reflect the values of our culture? The quality of family and community life?

3. When the expressed wishes of the deceased do not fit the needs of the surviving family, what options do survivors have?

4. Is the body the "temple of the Holy Spirit" or "just a shell"?

(Note: For a comparison of funeral costs in England in the 1800s with today's deathcare spending in the U.S., see Appendix E.)

Five

"Is There a God?"

God is our refuge and strength,
an ever present help in trouble …

Psalms 46:1

Ubi caritas et amor
Deus ibi est
(Where there is love and caring
There God is.)

When a loved one dies, many people question the existence of a divine being. But the question has really been around much longer. Questions about the existence of a higher power are so basic to life that our literature is organized around them. Melvil Dewey, originator of the Dewey Decimal System, chose his main subject groups by imagining a prehistoric person asking questions about the world:

100 *Who am I?*
   (Philosophy—books about one's mind and thoughts)
200 *Who made me?*
   (Religion, Bible stories and mythology)
300 *Who is the person in the next cave?*
   (Sociology—group relations, government, careers, customs, holidays, folklore, and fairy tales)
400 *How can I make that person understand me?*
   (Language, grammar, and spelling)

500 *What makes things happen in the world around me?*
(Science—animals, flowers, rocks, stars)
600 *How can I use what I know about nature?*
(Applied Science—invention, medicine,
engineering, manufacturing, and food)
700 *How can I enjoy my leisure time?*
(Arts and Recreation—hobbies, sports, music, theater,
art, and sports)
800 *What are the stories of human thoughts and deeds?*
(Literature—fiction, poetry, plays)
900 *How can I record what people have done?*
(History—biography, geography, and history)
000 *General Works*
(Reference)

The question of a higher power comes early in the Dewey organizational system. In Western culture's busy schedules, matters of faith may not get much attention. But in times of trouble—such as when a loved one dies, or there are human tragedies or natural disasters—most people turn instinctively to a higher power. During major life transitions such as graduating, getting married, having a new baby, or taking office in organizations, people pray, participate in religious rituals, and take oaths on the Bible. The sage who wrote "for everything there is a season" concludes that God has put eternity within human hearts (Ecclesiastes 3:11), and Jesus said, "The kingdom of God is among you (Luke 17:21, NRSV)." Spirituality, though not so visible, is a natural part of human existence.

God may be known by many names in many different languages and cultures. Some who are healing from religious confusion or spiritual abuse may find it helpful to use other names for the Holy One, such as The One-Who-Is, Love, Wisdom, Truth, Great Spirit, Good Shepherd, Higher Power, Yahweh, or El Shaddai.

While I haven't read all the books in the 200 section of the library and cannot offer scientific proof of the existence of a higher power, I can share a bit of the process I use, the experiences of some who have shared their stories and insights with me, and some of my reflections from living in a funeral home.

Before working in funeral service and going to seminary, I grew up in a faith tradition that involved me sitting quietly in the pew or singing psalms, memorizing and regurgitating Scripture (King James Version) and absorbing doctrinal teachings. All the while I wondered about many things: for example, why the faith presented in Sunday School songs— "Jesus Loves Me" and "Jesus Loves All the Children of the World"—was so different from the pulpit version of a jealous God who thundered out the Ten Commandments, finger-wrote them in stone, was also a warrior king, an austere judge (parent authority-figure substitute, patriarch-in-the-sky) who never slept but watched every move everyone made, ready to zap at the slightest offense, and most of all was the forbidder of pleasure (movies, dancing, and sexual activity).

This same God, both "Love" and "Judge-Forbidder," also created the sun, moon, stars, trees, animals, birds, fish and, at great risk, people with free will—who soon misused their freedom—which was good for endless guilt trips, especially for women because Eve ate the forbidden fruit before Adam. Meanwhile, the psalms were heartcries of oppressed people in their times of trouble—people who spoke directly with God and received justice, mercy, and equity, which were God's inherent attributes. As recipients of God's lovingkindness and tender mercies, they gave joyful thanks and praise to God.

Closer to God in the Garden

Considering these confusing messages, I felt closest to God on the back forty acres of the farm, climbing trees, watching the birds, watching the corn grow, enjoying long times of reflection alone. For me, Wisdom spoke profoundly in nature, and I wove Wisdom with the other messages I had received about God.

When I was in high school, a new mixed message was added: a yellow Q&A catechism book that posed the question: "Why do we not have miracles today like those in Bible times?"

And the "proper" answer: "Because the testimony of God has been sufficiently revealed." Such a deal! So God wasn't capable of delivering miracles anymore and the church fathers were covering! All the good stuff happened before I was born! Or in faraway lands the missionaries told about. But never here and now. And I was supposed to be content with that and tithe to the church for this information? Was God dead as some claimed? Was faith in God a form of mythology? A crutch to help weak people through life?

Working through Gender Issues

And why was this God so hard on women? I wondered why men made all the decisions and rules while women were relegated to cooking, cleaning, secretarial work, nursing, teaching, bearing and raising children—all without voice or vote in church matters that directly affected them. Their roles didn't look like much fun to me, and I wondered why they put up with it. When I heard a preacher bellowing "He shall do this and shalt not do that," I remember inwardly discounting: "That doesn't apply to me because I'm not a *he*."

When I asked questions about women's roles in the church, my questions were labeled "women's issues" and shelved as if they were not important Christian or human issues. I felt a lot of anger—and rage—about this. Eventually I discovered that my place of pain, anger, or passion was also my growing place. I found books that posed questions like mine, and I read the Bible for myself, discovering new approaches, insights, and ways to understand passages that had been troublesome.

I learned that the ancient Hebrew worldview included birthing—with the earth connected to Mother God by an umbilical cord attached at Mt. Zion, the earth's navel. From the beginning both "male and female" were created "in the image of God" (Genesis 1:27). The first human was without gender; gender differences were created simultaneously.[1]

Psalm 139 says all of us were on the mind of God before Creation began, and God knits each of us together in our mother's womb. Mary prophesied that the messianic mission was to bring down the mighty and lift up the lowly (Luke 1:51–53), bringing justice and equality to earth. When God became a person, the first nine months were lived in a woman's body, beginning as female like all human fetuses. So the divine order is really woman-child-man; and Jesus is man-born-of-woman, which includes all people. Heavenly beings and earthly shepherds sang together that the purpose of the holy birth was to give glory to God and bring peace (not war) on earth. (Luke 2:14)

Jesus is both Sophia/Wisdom-from-on-high and Word-of-God-Incarnate. Jesus called God *Abwoon*, which is Aramaic for Mother/Father, Birther/Creator, Source of our Heartbeats and our Lifebreath.[2] Aramaic, the language Jesus spoke, was the "traveler's" language, the one everyone understood, or as we might say today, the "inclusive" language of the day. In keeping with prophecies and the messianic mission, Jesus broke patriarchal tradition where it was oppressive to women, children, and men. Jesus called a crippled woman to the center of the synagogue on the Sabbath and healed her, breaking ancient taboos that forbade men to speak to women in public, barred women from the center of the temple, and prohibited any work—even merciful work—on the Sabbath (Luke 13:10–17). At the garden tomb on resurrection morning, Jesus appeared first to the women who had come to properly prepare his body for burial—and commissioned them as the first witnesses of the resurrection, pinnacle of the Christian faith.

Accordingly, women were bishops in the early church; there was even a woman pope. In time however, women's teachings were again suppressed, their writings deliberately destroyed, and their voices silenced by violence and a peculiar incongruity—the absolutizing of the Bible's patriarchal culture rather than the central theme of Christianity and the earth's other major religions: "Do to others what you would have them do to you." (Matthew 7:12) The Apostle Paul reflected the Golden Rule when he said there is now no more male or female, for all are one in Christ (Galatians 3:28).

In my searching, wondering, and reading, I learned that it is possible to read the Bible through the lenses of the patriarchal culture and the values of power, control, and money. It is also possible to see the Bible's central figure, the Good Shepherd, leading with love, justice (equity), and mercy to places of peace and plenty for all.

Psalm 23 is the Scripture most often read at funerals. People instinctively turn to the "Shepherd Psalm" for comfort. It's a scene anyone can picture—a shepherd's annual cycle as well as a life cycle. One can enter the pastoral scene with imagination and meet with the Shepherd. In ancient Middle Eastern culture both women and men were shepherds, so the imagery of God as Shepherd includes maternal and paternal attributes. The Good Shepherd leads the flock to green pastures, still waters, right paths, through danger, providing a table in the presence of the enemy, and ultimately to places of peace and plenty. The Good Shepherd holds us fast (John 10), and in the end "nothing will be able to separate us from the love of God" (Romans 8:39). The Bible begins with a wise and wonderful creation (not the "guilt" or "sin" of the guilt-grace-gratitude or sin-salvation-service formulas), takes us through the fall and struggles of faith, and ends with a restored and redeemed creation (Revelation 21) and a place prepared for us (John 14:1–3).

As I pursued my own faith journey, I gradually moved from a fear-based to a love-based perspective of Scripture and life. My growth and discoveries were not always welcomed by religious insiders, but acquaintances and "strangers" (Hebrews 13:1–2) often approach me to talk about matters of faith or to officiate at services for their loved ones. This has led me to believe that the "holy catholic church" referred to in the Apostles' Creed truly can be anywhere and everywhere.

Professions of Faith in a Pizza Parlor

Once I was in a pizza parlor when a woman I'll call Jenny began chatting with me as we waited for pizza. Coincidentally, Jenny was going through a stressful job situation much like one I'd had, so we shared stories of jobs, stress, and coping. As I shared ways my faith had grown through a difficult time, Jenny shared a time when the Good Shepherd was nearly palpable to her. It was a time when she was a teenager, very ill and in the emergency room. A chaplain came by and asked if there was anything he could do for her. She said, "You could read me the Twenty-third Psalm." After he left she said, "I was hovering high above my body while the words of the Twenty-third Psalm were being repeated as if on an intercom, and a nurse was doing CPR on me! At one point the nurse cried out, 'We're losing her!'" Even though it was a frantic scene, Jenny said she felt so peaceful, as if she were in the arms of the Good Shepherd. When Jenny and her body were reunited, she told the ER staff everything they'd said and done. And she told me that ever since that time she was no longer afraid of death.

Jenny also told me that she had never before shared her experience with anyone. She worked in a competitive business office, and knew she would get a mental health label and lose her job if she shared anything so mystical. When I asked why she had shared it with me she said, "I used to think that God communicated only through certain people, but I've learned from you that God speaks to everyone." While I don't have a clue how I conveyed that, Jenny affirmed a central truth of Scripture and the Twenty-third Psalm: God walks and talks with each of us and leads us safely through the valley of the shadow of death to a place of goodness and mercy forever—in this life and beyond.

But if God really leads us safely through life, why do tragedies happen? Why doesn't everyone recover from illnesses and "live happily ever after" like Jenny did? I remember a time when a young woman was hit by a drunk driver and I was asked to officiate at her service. I acknowledged to her family that I knew of no "answers" as to *why* this happened that would bring comfort. But I could ask the question in a different way: "Where is God when things like this happen?"—and offer three stories for consideration.

The first was the story of Joseph (Genesis 37, 39–50), unfairly thrown into a pit by his brothers, sold as a slave, then wrongly imprisoned by his boss's wife's lies. Seventeen years later, when Joseph was vice-president of Egypt and in charge of the grain storage program, his brothers came to buy grain during a famine. Joseph then realized the "why" of his troubles. He said to his brothers, "Even though you intended to do harm to me, God intended it for good, in order to preserve a numerous people (Genesis 50:20, NRSV)."

When Daniel chose worship of God over worship of King Darius as per the king's decree, he was thrown into the lions' den, prepared to die for his faith. But during his long night in the pits, the lions' mouths were miraculously closed, and he was delivered and elevated to royalty (Daniel 6).

When Jesus was betrayed by a close friend and prominent religious people, he too was thrown into a pit, tortured, executed, and buried. On the third day he was raised, showing followers the way through death to new life beyond. The stories of Joseph, Daniel, and Jesus give assurance that *God is with us* even in the pits—working far more powerfully than we can ask or imagine.

While "the pits" and the "valley of the shadow of death" are not pleasant, they are necessary parts of life's journey. The idea of suffering to grow in faith does not fit well into the popular health-and-wealth "gospel" of today. Throughout the pages of holy writ, however, suffering is an expected and necessary part of growth in faith. Whether the suffering is caused by us or by someone else, or even when there is no apparent cause, it has a purpose. Suffering can build perseverance, character, and hope (Romans 5:3–4), help us depend on a higher power (II Corinthians 12:8–10), make us able to comfort others (II Corinthians 1:3–4), keep us from becoming conceited (II Corinthians 12:7), test and refine faith (I Peter 1:6–7, Job 23:10) or discipline us (Hebrews 12:1–12). People of faith may even suffer for doing what's right (II Corinthians 11:22–28, Matthew 5:10–12), or they may suffer for reasons known only to God, as Job did.

From Cancer and Death to Butterflies and Rebirth

The issue of suffering was difficult for Patricia, a middle-aged woman who was dying of cancer. When I first visited her, she was angry that a recent vote to legalize euthanasia had not passed. Euthanasia made more sense to her than suffering. She was sarcastic about spiritual matters, especially the faith tradition of her childhood. And she adamantly rejected the one-size-fits-all conversion experience her well meaning neighbors tried to impose on her.

With my encouragement, Patricia began to re-explore the faith tradition of her childhood. Over the next few months I brought in a pastor from that faith tradition. He joked with Patricia about the guilt trips of the church's past, helped her reframe her faith, and offered her the sacraments. For several months she enjoyed improved health. She attended church and even went on a weekend retreat.

Through stories from *Kitchen Table Wisdom*[3] by Rachel Naomi Remen and visits from social workers and counselors, Patricia resolved some of her initial fear, anger, and self-pity. She was able to see her remaining time as a gift and even joked about dying. She planted flowers in her garden. As much as she could, she made peace with family and friends. She shared with me a time she felt God's presence very near. It was after her mother, Marie, died and she was feeling very sad. She went to the cemetery, and while she was kneeling at her mother's grave, butterflies suddenly surrounded her and "fluttered away" her sadness, leaving her feeling light and joyous.

After Patricia's memorial service, held on the lawn at her home, several of her friends and I were enjoying snacks and sharing memories when two butterflies of a kind I'd never seen before flew in at an angle, intentionally passed through the middle of our group, then up, up, and away, leaving us feeling light and joyful. We looked at each other, remembered, and said, "Hi, Patricia and Marie."

Just as nature goes through annual seasons, faith may pass through many stages before reaching maturity. I believe these stages are "cycles," and the completed journey will in some way be connected to the earliest stage. Even if there are claims otherwise, as there were with Garth.

Inside an Atheist, Faith Takes Root

Garth was brought up in a very strict faith tradition that used frequent mention of hellfire and brimstone to keep adherents in line. He became a professor, lived alone for most of his adult life, enjoyed reading and studying, and claimed to be an atheist. In his senior years he had a seizure disorder and needed to be hospitalized from time to time. After a day or two he would call and ask John or me to bring books and personal effects from his house.

Garth wasn't very social, and he never came to funerals because most are faith-based. But one day he came to a funeral, the first at which I was officiating. We were concerned that he might be disruptive. Because the family had requested a nontraditional service, I simply told the story of the Good Shepherd caring for sheep, leading them safely through the valley to peace and plenty on the other side, giving his life for the sheep.

Two days later Garth rang the doorbell, came through the entry and into the kitchen, looked me in the eye and said, "Celia, I just want to tell you that's the best funeral message I ever heard! I really mean that, and I want to thank you." John and I realized this was way out of character for Garth. We wondered if he had gone off his medication and might be needing help soon. And we wondered why a simple message

on the Twenty-third Psalm would be so meaningful to someone who claimed to be an atheist.

In the months that followed, Garth was hospitalized again
and was said to be incoherent. But, when I brought his books
and glasses to him, he spotted me, came running down the
hall to meet me, hugged me as if I were his best friend, and
led me into his room. We talked about his room and personal
effects for a few minutes, and then he went back to roaming
the hallways. As I was leaving his nurse approached me curi-
ously and said, "Garth hasn't said a coherent phrase or sentence since he's been here, and I timed him at two minutes of
normal conversation with you. I'd really like to know, what
is your relationship to Garth?" I told the nurse about Garth's
surprising response to the funeral message and speculated that
he may have been turned off to religion which had been "im-
posed," but that perhaps he had responded to a story that left
the interpretation to the hearers. The nurse concurred.

From then on, whenever I met Garth on the street, I just
smiled and said hello. I never mentioned matters of faith to
him again.

When Garth died a few years later I shared this memory
with his daughter. She said, "You were wise to let the story
take root in him and not approach him directly about matters
of faith." "Atheism" seems to have been this brilliant man's
defense against overzealous religion and proselytizing. True
faith had always been deep within, growing in secret, called
forth by the simple story of the Good Shepherd.

The experiences of Jenny, Patricia, and Garth combined
with my experiences, theological studies, and view from inside the funeral home have shown me that God—especially
as the Good Shepherd—is knowing and knowable. To personally experience God's presence one may have to deal with
anger, sort through fear-and-control-based messages of childhood, look one's own death in the face, dialogue with others,

experience solitude in nature, and question assumptions and expectations of oneself and others.

It is work worth doing, for peace is its priceless reward.

Afterthoughts

1. A trilogy: Who am I? Why am I here? Where am I going?

2. Am I a human being on a spiritual journey or a spiritual being on a human journey?

3. Is there really a God? Or is belief in a higher power just another form of mythology people invent to make themselves feel good or to manipulate others?

4. Some ways to nurture faith: reading, gardening, journaling, (slowing) breathing, listening, walking in nature, looking up at the stars, meditation, religious rituals, and service to others. While some meet with God in quiet, rural, or reflective settings, others experience God in sports activities and in the city. Perhaps you'd like to choose one (or more) method(s) and check it out yourself.

Six

Is There Life after Death?

Do not let your hearts be troubled. Believe in God, believe also in me.
In my Father's house are many dwelling places, if it were not so, I would
have told you; for I go to prepare a place for you.
John 14:1-2, NRSV

Belief in an afterlife takes on greater importance when a loved one has died. Scripture, poetry, stories, music, and nature all offer hope, comfort, and assurance of heaven for family and friends.

Descriptions of an afterlife are found in the Bible's prophetic writings, the parables, and in the apocryphal writings. During Israel's exile, prophets offered hope of recreating Israel's great united monarchy in which everyone had a place to live, plenty to eat, peace, and safety. The author of Revelation wrote of thrones surrounded by robed saints, streets of gold, a sea of crystal, a holy and peaceful city with trees and a river running through it.

I must confess that streets of gold and a sea of crystal have little appeal for me. I prefer the scenic two-track roads, lakes, and streams of northern Michigan. While gold and crystal may be pretty, walking on velvet would be much more fun. My concept of heaven would include the equality of which

Mary spoke (Luke 1:52), a restored Eden, a community in which everyone's needs are met and there is peace with God, self, others, and nature.

Perhaps the real test of anyone's concept of an afterlife is explaining it to a child. When our son Paul asked questions at the age of five, I told him, "Heaven is the most wonderful thing you can imagine, and then it's even better!" A little vague, perhaps, but an invitation to engage his imagination. After all, how could anyone believe in a place they've never seen without using their imagination?

This vague-but-imaginative concept of heaven served Paul fairly well until one Sunday a guest minister told a story about heaven. Someone who was struggling to understand the concept of heaven was taken on a tour by Elijah. Elijah led the student down a hall and into a room where a banquet table was laden with colorful and delicious foods of every kind, but those sitting around it looked unhappy and starved. The student said, "I don't understand." Elijah said, "Look again." Then the student noticed splints on their elbows preventing them from getting the food to their mouths. "OK," the student said. "So this is hell."

Elijah said, "Come and I will show you heaven." They went across the hall to another room with the same scenario: a banquet table richly laden with food and people with splints on their elbows. Except these people looked happy and well nourished. "I don't understand," said the student. Elijah said, "Watch."

The student watched as the people lifted their hands and gave thanks for the food. Then they reached across the table and fed each other. "Aha!" said the student, and Elijah affirmed, "This is heaven."

That Sunday, when Paul got home he faced me angrily, "Is what that preacher said about heaven and hell really true?"

I tried to explain that it was a story about the difference be-tween heaven and hell, but Paul wasn't buying it. He said, "You told me heaven was the best thing you could imagine and then it was even better. Well, *I like to swim, and you can't swim with splints on your elbows!*"

In that moment Paul's concept of heaven went the way of Santa, the Easter bunny, and the tooth fairy. So did my illu-sions about being able to "explain heaven" to a child.

Perhaps there were more concrete examples of heaven I could offer to Paul. I looked again at the stories Jesus told. They spoke of ordinary things like seasons and seeds but still invited the imagination to leap from the familiar to the less familiar concept of heaven. Perhaps nature's most concrete example of an afterlife is the caterpillar that pupates in a co-coon and later emerges as a butterfly. Nature's ongoing cycle of birth–death–rebirth offers clues to the mystery of an after-life.

Besides seeing evidence of heaven in nature, many peo-ple have had extraordinary personal experiences that have convinced them of an afterlife. Those who have shared their stories with me usually begin, "I've never told anyone this before … " They tell me of near-death, beyond-and-back, and other extraordinary experiences. Perhaps I'm a "safe" au-dience because I've sometimes taken the risk of sharing a personal experience.

Evidence of Things Unseen

After a deeply disappointing job experience, I worked with John one summer, mowing and trimming in the cemetery. One day as I trimmed grass around my Grandpa's and Grand-ma's stones, I noticed the month, day, and year of my Grandma's birth and death. She had died on August 31, exactly thirty-one years from the day I was standing there. Since I was a baby when she died, I was thirty-one years old at the time of this occurrence.

As I knelt beside their headstones in awe of this extraordinary coincidence, I recalled vividly a certain look on my grandpa's face. It had come at a time when I was perhaps four years old, tagging along with my grandpa and uncle while they were "fixin' fence." The sun was hot, so I had wandered over to some trees and sat in their shade. I have no idea how long I was there, but I remember Grandpa looking quite worried when he found me. He asked, "Weren't you afraid the bears would get you?" And I had answered, "No, God will take care of me." Then there was "that look" on Grandpa's face. The memory of that look recalled for me the faith that was mine as a child—faith that I needed now during my time of loss.

This experience—was it a coincidence, or was it something more?—changed my focus from grieving to action. I researched my roots. I searched for a picture of Grandma holding me. As I sorted through old pictures, I finally found a photo of Grandma sitting on the lawn with my sister and me. Grandma was reaching over my sister, her hands supporting me as a baby just learning to sit. I turned the picture over. On the back were some processing numbers—a 1 and a 3. I later discovered my grandpa's funeral message was based on Psalm 31. My mother was thirty-one when my grandma died. Someone suggested I find out what my grandma was doing when she was thirty-one. I dug some more and discovered that she had a kindergartner and four preschoolers, the youngest being twins who required much care, so perhaps this was a time of spiritual growth in her life also.

I talked with people who knew my grandparents. I wrote to the pastor who officiated at my grandma's funeral. He replied, saying he didn't know much about numerology or co-incidences, but on the basis of my letter he encouraged me to develop and use my writing ability. I exchanged letters with a couple of my great-uncles who were theologians and pastors.

Many people with whom I shared the experience offered suggestions and encouraged me to pursue its meaning. Others said, "I don't believe in such things." Some expressed concern for my mental health. Still others suggested I exploit the experience and play the lottery.

From research I learned that extraordinary coincidences involving numbers are also known as synchronistic events. Marie-Louise von Franz, a follower of Carl Jung, studied them and concluded that synchronistic events are "airholes to eternal life" or "windows open to eternity," which enable one to escape the stifling clutches of a one-sided view of life. Through this "window" one touches the eternal within oneself, and the eternal can reach into the human time-bound world. The interpretation of such an event belongs to the recipient.[1]

In the years that have followed, I have had similar experiences. Or perhaps these events are always occurring, but I only noticed them after I learned to pay attention. As I became receptive, people shared their stories with me. Following are some of the stories that I consider authentic because the recipients were cautious in sharing them and have not exploited them.

A Hard-Headed "Hard Hat"

One who shared his story quite freely was Burt, a construction worker with a quick temper. He says it didn't take much for him to "fly off the handle." One day while he was at work, he had heavy-duty chest pain, "like an elephant on my chest,"

as he described it. On the way to the hospital in the ambulance the pain became unbearable. He said, "I cried out to
God and asked him to take me or whatever, but take away
the pain.

"What happened next is 'unexplainable,'" he said. "The
best I can describe it is that the pain was gone, and I felt at
ease. I was wrapped in protection, the shadow of death. There
was light and peace, tranquility, and it was so beautiful that I
didn't want to come back. This must have taken just a short
time, and then the elephant was back on my chest." He remembers an ambulance intercept, being hooked up to an IV,
receiving medication to ease the pain, and the rest of the trip
to the hospital.

When I asked Burt what this experience meant to him, he
said, "I was like most people. I believed in God and an afterlife,
but I had some doubts. I knew I was going to die but wasn't
looking forward to it. I was in some ways afraid of death. After
that experience I'm still the 'rascal' I always was, but I don't
doubt anymore. I was shown what could be, and the choice
is up to me. I don't get angry anymore. When people bug
me, I forgive them and move on. The difference is my way of
thinking. My temper is something that's wrong with *me*, not
with them.

"My fears ain't fears no more. I was here, then there, and
somehow my fears and doubting and temper were 'absorbed.'
My whole outlook on life is different. I don't fear death—
only how it may happen."

I asked Burt how his experience changed his relationships
with others, he said, "It's easier to talk to my kids and grand-
kids now. I know everyone doubts, and young people doubt a
lot. By telling young people what I experienced it gives them
a handhold, an assurance. I'm ready, willing, able, and available
for whatever God has planned for me.

"I didn't see angels or anybody who had gone on before. I was just given a look—shown what could be—but I also came to understand that God wasn't finished with me. The impact of the experience is up to me. I've decided to tell others what's there for them also, so they can decide better. I was shown a chance, not a guarantee—given a do-with-it-what-you-will experience. I cried out, and I know God is only a prayer away."

Burt says of himself, "When you're hard-headed, God has got to show you." To others who doubt or need an experience of God's nearness or hope of heaven, Burt says, "Just cry out."

"Crying out" may seem a foreign idea in a "keep-a-stiff-upper-lip" culture where people are encouraged to move on quickly after trauma or loss. But the ancient Hebrew people knew much about crying out to God. They knew it as their privilege and responsibility. Over half the Psalms are songs of lament. Crying out to God cleanses the soul of anger, envy, grief; it puts the pain in God's hands and creates an empty place in the heart—room for more grace, mercy, peace, love and joy.

Walter Brueggeman lists six parts of a lament:

1. *Addressing God by name, "My God"*
2. *Pouring out the complaint*
3. *Offering the petition*
4. *Giving reasons why God "should" act as requested*
5. *Requesting vengeance on the enemy (putting "revenge" in God's hands). After fully voicing the hurt or need, "something unexpected happens in the psalm. The mood and tone of the psalm change."*
6. *The lament ends in rejoicing and praise.*[2]

A Grandmother Hangs On—Then Lets Go

While Burt was open and forthcoming with his experience, Merla kept her feelings and deepest doubts inside. She had struggled with cancer for a few years and was near death when she asked me to come and see her. When I asked if she was ready to go to heaven, Merla said wearily, "I hope so." Her family and I longed to hear an "I know so."

On my next visit to the hospital I found Merla too weak to speak, so I asked questions she could answer by nodding yes or no. I asked if she was angry with God for not letting her stay and watch her grandchildren grow up, and Merla nodded yes. I asked, "Would you like to hear a story about two women who got mad at God?" Another nod. I read John 11:1–45 with emphasis on Mary and Martha each scolding Jesus for not coming when they called for him, "*Lord, if you had been here,* my brother (Lazarus) would not have died!" (verses 21 and 32, italics mine). I asked, "Did you notice God didn't fall out of heaven or zap Mary and Martha because they got mad at Jesus?" Merla smiled. I said, "You can silently tell God what you're angry about; God will hear and answer you." I left for a while to let the process work.

When I returned I asked, "Did you and God get everything worked out?" She nodded enthusiastically. "Do you know for sure that God has a place for you in heaven?" Another enthusiastic nod. Then for reasons I can't explain I asked Merla, a woman too weak to talk or open her eyes, for a hug. To her husband's and my amazement, she reached up with both arms and wrapped them tightly around my neck, conveying with all her strength her assurance of a place in heaven—perhaps with a window through which she could watch her grandchildren grow up—or wings to wear so that she could be with them in new ways.

Roughneck Factory Worker

I don't know if Merla got a glimpse of what lies ahead as Burt did. But Rudy did. Rudy was a factory worker, married with children, a churchgoer who did not treat his wife and children well. After the children were grown, Rudy had a heart attack during which he had an out-of-body experience. He told his family he actually entered heaven, walked its streets, looked in the windows, and saw people who had gone before him. But, instead of staying there, Rudy returned to his earthly body. He reflected on his life and on his experience of walking the streets of heaven. Then he changed the way he lived. He treated his wife and children with new respect and consideration. Whenever he had the opportunity, he told people that God and heaven are real.

Many who knew Rudy previously were skeptical of the change in his life. Some found him downright annoying. They predicted the change wouldn't last. As one probation officer says, "I've never seen so many people find the Lord so fast when they're in trouble and then forget about God even faster once they're out of trouble." But the change in Rudy's life lasted many years after his beyond-and-back experience—a testament to its authenticity and purpose.

An Old Man Heals the Hurt Child Inside

Just as everyone's life experiences are unique, their ideas of what an afterlife is like may also vary. Aaron was an adult foster care resident who was in the hospital's intensive care unit and near death when I was asked to visit him. As I rode to the hospital with Martha, his caregiver, I learned Aaron's story.

Soon after he was born, Aaron's parents decided he "wasn't school material," so he was "worked" on the farm. He was a good worker, so other farmers "used" him also. Some abused him. Some made sport of him. They wrapped him in barbed wire and left him sitting helplessly in a field. Sometimes the barbed wire was connected to an electric fence, and they threw water on him. Aaron was embarrassed about this and revealed it only when a trusted caregiver asked what caused the little red marks on his arms.

When Aaron was sixty-two and living in a musty basement, Gail, a social worker, found out about his situation. She drove him to various adult care homes and let him pick the one he liked best, Martha's Place. After all Aaron's possessions were unloaded from the trunk of Gail's car, Martha washed and washed the clothes but could not get rid of the musty smell. Finally, she threw them away and bought new clothes for him. Aaron wept when he received the new clothes, as he would weep many times thereafter whenever anyone did something kind for him—baked him a birthday cake or gave him a birthday or Christmas present.

Martha's Place was "like heaven" for Aaron. Martha's children and their friends loved him as a grandpa. He always had time for them and would play games or toss a ball as long as they wanted. If he didn't greet them when they visited, they'd go looking for him and climb in his lap.

So when Martha and I arrived in the ICU, she told Aaron how much she and her family and friends loved him. As I affirmed God's love for him, I told him the place God had prepared for him was even better than Martha's Place.

Letty and the Angels

While many who are dying cannot tell us what they see or hear, some see heavenly beings or loved ones who have gone on before them. This happened for Letty, an elderly woman who was dying at home. After I read Scripture and prayed with her, Letty suddenly opened her eyes and looked directly at me. But her eyes were not really seeing me; they were looking beyond. She started talking to someone, and I asked her who she was talking to. "The angels!" she said. "Can't you see them?" Letty talked to the angels for three days, weaving heaven and earth together for her family, until she went peacefully to the house of "many rooms" (John 14:2), a house "not made with hands, eternal in the heavens" (II Corinthians 5:1, KJV).

Lisa and the Light

It isn't only those who are "old and full of years" who see heavenly beings. Lisa was a young woman dying of injuries sustained in an accident. As her family stood around her bed, Lisa suddenly said, "Who's that?" She pointed to the foot of her bed where no one was standing. "He's all shiny!" Her mother said, "Lisa, that's Jesus." Nurses in a nearby wing of the hospital later confirmed that they saw a "bright shaft of light" entering Lisa's room at that time—on a very overcast day.

A Boy Becomes a Disciple

Benton was another young person with an extraordinary experience. He was five years old when he fell out of a tree and hit his head on a stone. As he was dying, his family surrounded his bed and prayed. A shining being the family identified as Jesus appeared at the foot of his bed. Then, instead of dying, Benton recovered. Benton grew up and became a farmer. He prayed daily and faithfully attended church. One day while he was praying he felt a severe pain in his hands. He looked down to see a circle in the middle of each palm, open and bleeding—something known as *stigmata*. Benton discovered that many experienced healing as he prayed for them. One day while he was in prayer, God told him to use this gift to love, bless, and heal people. Benton retired as a farmer and traveled at his own expense, refusing any offerings or payment, teaching forgiveness, and blessing and healing people.

A Divorced Mom Musters her Faith

Besides previews of heaven or seeing shining beings, belief in the afterlife is affirmed for some when they receive visits from relatives who have died. Meg, mother of four, was going through a long, difficult, and complicated divorce. With each court appearance and contested detail she grew more and more weary. One day, when she was not at work and the children were in school, she felt on the brink of despair. In a surreal moment, her grandparents, who had died years earlier, appeared in the living room with her, reassuring her: "It's going to be all right." As they lingered, her despair lifted. From that visit she drew the strength, hope, and assurance she needed to go on living, working, and raising her children.

A Teacher with No Time for Goodbye

Everett, a teacher, also received a visit from beyond. He and his wife Lara were middle aged when Lara died suddenly of a brain hemorrhage. There was no time to say goodbye, and this was the most difficult part of his grief. A few weeks later, in the middle of the night, Everett turned over and saw Lara in bed with him. She spoke no words, just gazed at him lovingly,

radiantly, and peacefully. That look gave him the assurance
that Lara was in a peaceful and happy place and that he would
see her again one day. Everett now works as a counselor, offering assurance and hope to others.

A Frazzled Mom Finds Comfort

Karmen, a young mother, lived with her husband and children
far away from the farm where she had grown up. In the weeks
and months following her mother's death, she often felt overwhelmed with grief. She had hoped to watch her mom enjoy
being a grandma and to return to the farm for more visits
with her mom. One day while Karmen was in her apartment,
the phone rang. She answered and heard her mom's voice
saying, "Karmen, don't worry so much. I'm OK." While this
was comforting, it was also perplexing. Karmen wished they
could have talked longer and she could have found out more
about her mother's new life.

A few months later on a rainy day, Karmen's baby Ian was
very fussy. She gave him a bottle, changed his diaper, held
and rocked him, but he continued to cry. Just when she was
exasperated and at her wit's end, Karmen heard her mom's
voice saying clearly, "Put him in the high chair so he can look
outside and watch the rain." She followed those instructions
and Ian stopped fussing.

Karmen's Mom had had a favorite song, "One Day at a
Time," which she sang and played every day, especially after
being diagnosed with cancer. One day Karmen and her family went with her brother and his family to an amusement
park together. As they entered the cafeteria where recorded
secular music was playing, they heard the song, "One Day at
a Time."

Perhaps there are scientific or psychological explanations for the events I've described. Or perhaps death and grief can open our eyes to hidden, invisible spiritual truths. Perhaps that is the aim of the author of the "faith hall of fame" (Hebrews 11) and the verse that follows: "Therefore, since we are surrounded by so great a cloud of witnesses, let us also lay aside every weight and the sin that clings so closely, and let us run with perseverance the race that is set before us" (Hebrews 12:1, NRSV). Or, "Do not neglect to show hospitality to strangers, for by doing that some have entertained angels without knowing it" (Hebrews 13:2, NRSV). Or, "I will never leave you nor forsake you" (Hebrews 13:5c, NRSV).

To believe means to "act as if" invisible truths such as an afterlife and heavenly beings are real (Hebrews 11:1–2). By believing, earth becomes more "as it is in heaven" (Matthew 6:10), giving meaning and fullness to life here and now and taking "the sting" out of death (I Corinthians 15:51–58).

Besides the many biblical references to heaven, I like the way a couple of old hymns affirm the afterlife: A verse of "The Church's One Foundation" begins, "Yet we on earth have union with God, the Three-In-One, *and mystic sweet communion with those whose rest is won.*" The hymn, "For the Beauty of the Earth" contains the phrase, "Friends on earth and friends above," as if there is no separation.

The wise author of Ecclesiastes (3:11, NIV) looks at life from the outside and inside and says that God "has set eternity in the hearts" of all. Perhaps like homing pigeons humans have an inner instinct which leads them safely "home."

Afterthoughts

1. What experiences have you had that make heaven real to you?

2. What experiences of family and friends have made heaven real to them?

3. Describe your concept of heaven or an afterlife.

Seven

WHERE DOES ONE BEGIN TO PLAN A FUNERAL?

So teach us to number our days,
that we may apply our hearts unto wisdom.

Psalm 90:12, KJV

After a glimpse of life inside a small-town funeral home, you may be wondering: Where does one begin in planning a funeral? What options are available? What decisions need to be made?

This book offers two ways to go at this point:

1. *Appendix A is a flow chart with references to other appendices—information condensed for immediate use.*
2. *Or, for more ideas and stories, read on.*

One of the more creative funeral planners we've known is Aunt Annie. While many might approach funeral planning by talking with family and friends, reading up on the subject, calling funeral homes for price information, and assessing their resources, Aunt Annie had her own unique approach.

Since she was a widow without children, Aunt Annie's closest kin were her nieces and nephews. She didn't have a lot of money, and she didn't want to burden her family with her final expenses, so she set up a partially funded pre-need account. Every couple of months she would call John and tell him she had an extra $100 or $200 to add to her account. Since she didn't drive, she invited him to come over for tea. "Tea" lasted no less than an hour. Aunt Annie would bring on the tea and cookies. While John was sipping and munching she would describe the grand way she wanted her family and friends to celebrate her life after she died. Before the tea and cookies were finished, Aunt Annie went back into the kitchen for second helpings—to buy more time and elaborate on the details of her service. As her plan progressed she discovered that, if she didn't have money to add to her account, she could have a tea party anyway—changing some detail about the service to make the house call seem more legitimate.

The tea parties continued for several years until Aunt Annie got the account built up to cover the cost of a modest funeral. Soon thereafter Aunt Annie went into a nursing home where there was a ready-made social life, and someone else planned the tea parties.

When Aunt Annie died a few years later, her pastor designed the funeral service around her favorite Scripture and hymns. At one point he mentioned how Aunt Annie always served tea and cookies when she confided her funeral plans to him. Laughter rippled through the chapel as we all realized Aunt Annie had "confided" her funeral plans to *everyone* over tea and cookies! One can only guess the amount of tea and cookies Aunt Annie's plan required.

Aunt Annie's service took place on a cold and blustery winter day. About thirty of her family and friends attended. Her family provided a grand luncheon, and to keep everyone warm and cozy we hosted the luncheon in our home. The luncheon was a great tribute to those tea-and-cookie parties of yore.

Aunt Annie's financial plan worked well. Her pre-need account drew interest, which more than covered her funeral expenses. There was enough for some flowers besides.

Since not everyone has the time (or desire) for the tea-party plan, there are other ways to plan a funeral. But Aunt Annie had the right idea—a good place to start is by discussing end-of-life issues with family and close friends, provided the discussions go beyond jokes, glib answers, and denial. While talking about one's own funeral may be uncomfortable, it can clarify values and deepen family relationships, friendships, and faith. By discussing funeral plans before a death occurs, families can explore options, contact local funeral homes, and get price information when there are no time or distance constraints. Planning ahead simplifies details for survivors at a time when they may be under emotional stress.

Flexibility Foremost

Even when arrangements are made in advance, however, the next-of-kin have the right to change them. At death, one's body becomes the legal "property" of the next of kin. So in addition to one's own wishes, it's also important to ask, "What will family and friends need when I die?" Circumstances may change, or the needs of family and friends may differ from the time the plan was originally made to the actual time of death. Families usually do their best to honor the deceased's wishes and accommodate their own needs; however, providing some flexibility spares survivors from guilt should they need to make changes.

Prearrangements can be made with or without prefunding. Prefunding is advisable—and usually recommended by social workers and health caregivers—when someone goes into long-term care or when their closest relatives are not living nearby.

Needing a Better Goodbye

What can happen when there is inadequate planning? When Alan, an 85-year-old widower, died suddenly, some of his six children had had no contact with him for many years. Several weren't on good terms with him or with each other. Phil, Alan's son and main caregiver, had had power of attorney, but this ended at death. Even so, Phil took charge of the arrangements and decided on direct cremation without viewing or a service. Since all the children were equally the legal next-of-kin, each had to sign authorization forms for cremation. Although this can be done by fax, Alan's other five children drove long distances and straggled into the funeral home one at a time over the next thirty-six hours to sign forms—each protesting Phil's choices and expressing reluctance to sign.

John offered each of them an opportunity to see their father lying on a cot in the chapel; however, since Michigan law requires final disposition of an unembalmed body within forty-eight hours of death, there was little remaining time for the family to meet and make decisions. Since none of Alan's other children were willing to pay for the additional services they wanted, they reluctantly went along with the arrangements Phil had made, lingering as if hoping for something more. They left dissatisfied, making protests to John rather than to Phil.

Alan's five children anticipated that there would be plenty of resources available for their father's services, so they suspected Phil of mishandling their father's funds. This is a familiar story. But like many elderly persons, Alan's meager resources had been drained by healthcare costs. Had he gone into long-term care, or applied for assistance through SSI or Medicaid, a social worker would most likely have advised him or his family to preplan and prepay funeral expenses. With discussion and planning, Alan's family may have been able to meet their emotional, spiritual, and financial needs at the time of their father's death in spite of limited resources.

Share and Share Alike

Many families have financial circumstances no better than Alan's but manage to pay for the funeral services they want and need. The Wilkes family also had six grown children who lived some distance from their parents. When their father died, they all wanted a visitation and traditional funeral service in the hometown church, even though there was no insurance, savings or pre-need account. The Wilkes children discussed the situation briefly. Then they divided the total cost by six, and each of them signed the funeral agreement. Within two weeks we received six checks that completely covered the cost of the funeral.

With the Wilkes family, as with Alan's family, there was no advance planning, and economy was an important consideration. The Wilkes family, however, was in agreement about what they wanted and had a realistic financial picture. They balanced economy with emotional and spiritual needs and were satisfied with the services they selected. Alan's family may also have had the ability to pay for what they wanted and needed had they been able to talk with each other and make mutual decisions.

Careful Planning Repairs Old Rifts

Sometimes, when families preplan, things turn out better than they anticipated. The middle-aged Turners were proud people who always paid their bills. They wanted to preplan and prepay their final expenses to spare their seven grown children that task, but they hadn't been able to save as much as they had hoped. When they came to the funeral home to make prearrangements, they had saved a total of six thousand dollars and figured all they could afford was immediate cremation. So, John gave them prices for cremation. Then he asked if they had talked this over with their children. They hadn't. For comparison purposes, John gave them prices for two traditional funerals, using the lowest priced caskets and vaults. When they saw that their savings could grow to cover the cost of two traditional funerals, they said that was what they had really wanted but considered to be out of their reach financially.

When Mrs. Turner died suddenly several years later, the children all came, some from long distances. They had not been together as a family since the oldest child left home. Over the next three days they spent time together at the family home. They made a collage of photos to celebrate memories at the visitation. They worshiped together during the funeral at the church where they had grown up. They went to the cemetery together for the burial and ate together at a luncheon prepared by friends at the church. They reminisced, hugged, cried, laughed, and reconnected with each other and with relatives and friends they hadn't seen in years. After the funeral, two of the Turner children told us they had felt estranged from the family, but during the days they spent together they had found healing from hurtful times of the past. Spending time together after the death of their mother had

deepened family relationships and shown them the importance of family ties. They planned regular family gatherings
for the years to come.

Each family decides, actively or passively, what is most
important to them—whether it be relationships, spirituality,
time, or money. Actively planning makes it more likely that
families will get what they need and want.

Aunt Annie had her tea-party planning, Alan's family passively decided not to plan, the Wilkes family had a shared, at-
need plan, and the Turner family planned ahead and got more
than they expected. But I don't think anyone could ever have
been ready for Grandma Z's plan:

If You're Too Careful, You *Can* Take it with You!

Grandma Z was a very private farm woman. This was back in
the 1950s when many rural women designed and sewed their
own undergarments. A stock item was a corset with stitched-
in "stays" (boning) to keep its shape so it could help a woman
keep hers. When Grandma Z became ill, she took off her
homemade corset and flung it over the clothes rack before
going to the hospital. When she died a couple of weeks later,
her family brought the corset to the funeral home along with
her other clothing. (Yes, we do need underwear.)

As John's Dad was dressing her and had the corset almost
completely laced, he noticed a slight lump. Investigating further he found a savings passbook stitched between two of the
stays. Some stitching had to be removed to get it out. Then,
carefully checking between the other stays he found stocks,
bonds, and another savings passbook.

When Grandma Z's family was notified, they were flab-
bergasted. They knew nothing about her secret savings, stocks,

or bonds. Grandma Z had been so private about her planning that she almost took her money with her when she went!

During our early years in funeral service, some people set aside funds for their funeral expenses by purchasing a certificate of deposit at the bank, made payable upon death to the funeral home, and they furnished the funeral home with that information. At the time of death, the funeral director could receive payment from the bank by presenting a certified copy of the death certificate.

In 1984, however, the Federal Trade Commission made a rule regulating funeral service. It required that all pre-need funds be held in a trust account, with anticipated funeral expenses itemized in the agreement between the individual and the service provider. This requirement benefited both consumers and funeral homes, protecting pre-need funds from misuse by either. (For funeral homes, the ruling also meant an increase in paperwork, which increased the cost of doing business, which in turn was passed on to the consumer.) Establishing a trust for pre-need funds is usually advisable when a person goes into long-term care or needs to apply for Medicaid or SSI benefits.

Assets may legally be set aside for a funeral with a guaranteed price agreement, and these can be certified irrevocable by the ruling social service agency. All assets that are certified irrevocable must be used for funeral expenses and cannot be returned to the family. However, pre-need accounts that are *not* certified irrevocable can be changed as needed or returned to the family. Both revocable and irrevocable accounts can be transferred to another funeral home.

The 1984 ruling also required funeral homes to present their itemized price list before discussing merchandise and to give price quotes by phone or in person upon request. For consumers this means the right to call funeral homes and

comparison shop. After choosing a funeral home, one can select goods and services (it's a good idea to take along a family
member or trusted friend), provide the funeral home with
information that will be needed for the death certificate and
obituary, discuss payment options, and ask questions—with or
without prefunding.

Besides pre-need trust accounts, funerals can be prepaid
with life (or death) insurance (policies can be certified irrevocable), annuities, or by setting up a prepayment plan (*see Appendix E*). A $255 Social Security benefit is payable to the sur-
viving spouse only. There may be Veterans benefits. If someone
dies and has no estate, the state may pay a specified amount
and family members can supplement. The amount that our
state currently pays does not cover the funeral home's out-of-
pocket costs. Sometimes the family divides the cost of the funeral or sets up a payment plan. Occasionally a family "angel"
pays. Sometimes the community holds fundraising events to
help with expenses.

Most families in our community realize that we're a small
business with high overhead and cannot continue to provide
services unless we receive payment. The need for funeral service can be sporadic. One year we went six months with no
income from the business. This was followed by three rather
busy years. Because of the fluctuating need, funeral homes are
usually bought and sold an average of every five years.

A Historical Perspective on Funeral Costs

Following the FTC rule enacted in 1984, funeral homes must
itemize their charges and provide pricing information upon
request—before showing or discussing the sale of merchandise. This rule makes it possible for consumers to price shop.

Funeral homes may also offer a "funeral service package" price, the service charge for a traditional funeral service. Service charges are based on the funeral home's cost of doing business and are not negotiable. Costs of caskets, vaults, and urns vary.

National averages of funeral costs do not include burial costs, which can vary greatly—cost of plot, vault, grave opening and closing, use of a tent and equipment. (*See Appendix E for a General Price List.*)

Below is a comparison of funeral costs in England in the 1800s, which was published in an article by Oliver McRae in *The Director*, with McRae's comments:

We live in the most affluent time in all of human history. More people have more money and are spending it more freely than ever before. Yet the following true story has become the dominant picture of the deathcare industry today:

A wealthy American couple drives up to a memorialist's office in a $90,000 automobile. They get out wearing designer clothing and jewelry of equal value. They go in, sit and, for the next hour, haggle about spending more than $5,000 for a memorial.

Contrast the above condition with an economic analysis delivered to the English parliament in 1844. Deathcare spending averages (here translated into dollars by the author), per person, for Europe were:

$1,000–$3,000 for a nobleman
$400–$800 for upper class, non-nobility
$500 for a gentleman
$120–$200 for an upper tradesman

Using historical conversion tables, their equivalent value for the year 2005 would be:

$193,000–$580,000 for "old money," CEOs, and
  industry leaders
$77,500–$155,000 for upper management,
  doctors, and lawyers
$96,900 for small-business owners
$23,250–$38,500 for middle management,
  teachers, and administrators[1]

Planning one's own funeral is an act of faith and courage. Preparing for its cost through prearrangement with a funeral service or savings account whose earnings keep pace with inflation is an act of love and consideration for one's survivors. People often plan for things that never happen, save for rainy days that never come, and insure against risks that never occur. A funeral fund is one savings account that *will* be put to use.

Afterthoughts

1. What advantages are there to preplanning a funeral?

2. When family members have different needs and expectations at a time of loss, what options do they have?

3. Review Appendix E and estimate what today's costs would be for a funeral of your choice. How can you begin to plan for that now?

Eight

How Does One Work
with a Funeral Director?

Lord, let me know my end, and what is the measure of my days;
let me know how fleeting my life is.

Psalm 39:4, NRSV

When I asked my husband John this question, he replied, "Have some idea of what you want. A lot of people don't want to talk about death and funerals, but death happens on a regular basis whether one is prepared or not. And when it does, people have to make lots of decisions in a short time. It's easier to serve people who have some idea of what they want."

Some people do know exactly what they want! One day while John was on a ladder painting the front of the house, an elderly couple pulled up beside the curb. The man got out and called up to John, "Are you the funeral director?"

"Yes, I am."

"Do you sell funerals to people who aren't dead yet?"

"I sure do."

"Then I'd like to buy two of them."

John came down from the ladder and invited the Parkers inside. He showed them a general price list, and they signed a form acknowledging that John had given them a general price list before showing or discussing merchandise. These first steps are required by the FTC. Since we don't have a showroom, John showed the Parkers pictures of caskets and vaults: they selected caskets and vaults and signed guaranteed price agreements. They provided information needed for death certificates and obituaries. After they wrote checks to the funeral home, John wrote checks to set up two trust accounts through a third party escrow agent. When Mrs. Parker entered a nursing home some years later, the guaranteed price agreement was certified as irrevocable by Michigan's Department of Human Services. When Mrs. Parker died, John faxed a copy of the death certificate to the trust agency and received a check for the original amount, plus interest.

While funeral directors can legally charge for pre-need conferences or setting up pre-need accounts, many do not. Also, if there is an excess, funeral directors can legally keep it; but, again, many do not. If the guaranteed price agreement has been certified irrevocable, the excess must be used for funeral expenses; it cannot be refunded to the family. John has used excesses to pay for airline tickets, family floral arrangements, and funeral luncheons; or he has donated the balance to a charity chosen by the family.

One of the first decisions a family must make is the choice of a funeral director or funeral home. In a small town such as ours with a second-generation funeral director, most people know the "undertaker" personally. Many in our village have known John since birth. Some were his babysitters who tell stories about him, such as the one about the way his mother curtailed his wandering by tying him to the front porch. When the neighbor kids teased, he told them, "This is my play rope." Some of the kids went home and asked their mothers to tie them to the porch!

Many also know John as a school bus driver. Even the children know that when John puts on a white shirt and goes away in the hearse it means someone has died.

John is also known from his service on the volunteer fire and rescue department. When the rescue service was called to Grandpa Henry's house because he appeared to be having a stroke, John checked his alertness by asking, "Do you know who I am?" Grandpa Henry shot back, "Yes, I do, and I'm not ready for you yet!"

Miss Nina also related to John in his funeral director role. Miss Nina enjoyed wearing colorful clothing and makeup. Whenever she saw John she'd say, "Remember, when I go, lots of rouge!" We attended a ninetieth birthday party for Miss Nina where she unwrapped a gift containing a red-print robe and matching slippers. Her family urged her to model them, but she said, "No, I'm saving these for John."

The First Steps

When a death occurs and the funeral home has been selected, one of the first things a funeral director will need to know is the method of disposition (burial, cremation, donation as in Appendix D) and whether there will be a visitation, if the casket will be open, and whether there will be a service. Embalming is required by Michigan state law if burial or cremation does not take place within forty-eight hours of death or if the body will be shipped by common carrier to another location. If embalming is to be done, the funeral director needs permission from the next of kin, and embalming should be done as soon as possible.

If cremation is chosen—with or without embalming, viewing, and funeral services—signatures of the next of kin and the medical examiner are required. Many medical examiners now charge fees for this service, and in our state these are payable at the county clerk's office at the time the death certificate is filed.

Often the funeral director will meet with the family—at their home or the funeral home—on the day of death or the following day. If the death has been sudden or if plans have not been made earlier, family members making arrangements may wish to bring a trusted friend to help with decision-making and details.

During this family conference, the funeral director will need information for completing the death certificate. This includes name as on birth certificate as well as current name and other names used, Social Security number (not always the same as Medicare), highest level of education completed, ancestry, mother's maiden name, and more (*see Appendix B*). Death certificates are redesigned every ten years or so, sometimes with input from funeral directors, sometimes not. The most recent Michigan certificate includes additional questions regarding ancestry, smoking, and pregnancy.

The funeral director will also need information for the obituary or death notice (*see Appendix C*) and in which newspapers the family wishes to publish this information.

At the time of need the funeral director also presents the family with a general price list and a form to sign acknowledging that they've seen it before viewing any merchandise such as caskets, vaults (required by most cemeteries), or urns.

For a funeral or memorial service the funeral director may ask where and when the family wishes the service to be held. Who will officiate? What music does the family want and whom do they wish to provide the music? Will the funeral director or family member contact the musicians? Some funeral homes employ organists, pianists, or other musicians.

Many also have a selection of recorded music. Some families prefer to provide their own music, live or recorded.

The funeral director may also ask: Will the casket be open before, during, or after the service? Will there be a procession to the cemetery? If there is to be a luncheon or dinner following the service, who will prepare and serve the meal? How many people should the dinner be prepared for? Where will it be held? Who will arrange for this? Will a nursery be provided? Some of these details may be worked out with the person who is officiating, particularly if the service is held in a church.

Does the family wish to designate a charity to receive memorial gifts? Often local charities are the most popular.

What to Bring for Preparing the Body

Clothing for the deceased should include underwear, socks, or stockings. Shoes are optional. Men don't need to wear suits and ties, and women don't need to wear dresses or skirts. Clothing may be as formal or as informal as the family wishes, even pajamas. Some families provide caps or hats, glasses, toothpicks (and even mints in a pocket for grandchildren to take). Children sometimes draw pictures or write notes to put in the casket. For a poker player, one family slipped a winning poker hand into the casket. Others put stuffed animals, pictures, flowers, or special trinkets in the casket as mementos. Some caskets come with memory drawers for that purpose.

If family members' wishes differ, it is often possible to accommodate many of their wishes. Funeral directors can sometimes offer options that haven't occurred to the family. Some funeral directors guide families through the decision-making process. Others ask for one family member with contractual

authority to act as spokesperson for the family. Sometimes it
is necessary for the family to gather elsewhere, make mutual
decisions, and have the contracting family member return to
the funeral home with clear instructions.

When a family is first presented with a general price
list (*see Appendix E*) it may not make a lot of sense. A family
may choose to go through the list item by item or select a
"funeral service package," the fee for which includes the funeral home's services for a traditional funeral, including the
staff's services, transportation, embalming, memorial package
(register book, folders, acknowledgment cards), visitation, funeral, and burial or cremation. Each funeral home calculates
its own service charge on the basis of its overhead, which includes taxes, insurance, vehicles, mortgage, rent, maintenance,
utilities, caskets, vaults, urns, office and general equipment,
supplies, and so forth. Each year in December our suppliers
send greetings—and new price lists. I don't recall the prices
ever going down.

Long-Distance Decisions

If someone dies far away from the funeral home they have
chosen, it's best to call the chosen funeral home first. This can
spare a family (and the funeral director) unnecessary hassles
and expenses. When Mr. Michaels died Friday in Texas, his
family called a funeral home there. Staff members removed
his body from the hospital, placed the body on the embalming table, and then left the funeral home for the weekend.
The family wanted a Monday visitation and a Tuesday funeral
at our funeral home. After many phone calls throughout the
day (and night), the family had to disengage the services of
the Texas funeral home before we could take official action.

John then engaged the services of a professional shipping firm, which engaged the services of another Texas funeral home to remove Mr. Michaels' body from the first home (with police assistance), embalm it, and ship it over the weekend so that the family could have a visitation and funeral as they had planned. To make the connection within that time frame required extensive ground travel as well as air travel.

When a loved one dies far from home, the family experiences stress in addition to grief and may be especially vulnerable. Some families have been told they need to purchase a casket for shipping by air. Since air freight charges are computed by weight, this adds to the shipping costs. In truth, all that is required is a lightweight wood/fiberboard container called a "shipping tray," which costs less than $100.

If Mr. Michaels had been cremated and his family had wished to take the cremated remains, known as cremains, on a flight to their hometown area, the cremains would have needed to be in a container through which x-rays can pass. Airport officials do not open cremation containers or handle cremains.

Survival Tips for Survivors

Even when a death is expected and planned for, there may be exhaustion from caregiving, missed meals, missed sleep, or an extended vigil. There may be a sense of loss as well as a sense of relief. There may be shock or numbness, especially when a death is sudden and unexpected. For any of these reasons, taking care of yourself is important—especially adequate rest and good nutrition.

Friends may offer help with practical tasks—providing meals, keeping a list of who brought what and in what kind of dish if the dish needs to be returned, answering the door and phone, making calls, doing laundry or cleaning, house sitting, or canceling meetings or appointments.

Sometimes families also have to keep the funeral director in line. We still chuckle at the time John was driving the hearse, leading a procession to the cemetery, talking with the minister who was riding with him, and missed the turn to the cemetery. The family member immediately behind the hearse stopped and allowed for correction. And John's dad recalled a time he led a procession to the cemetery for burial only to discover he had forgotten to order the vault.

Our funeral home is probably typical of those in many small towns. The funeral director is known personally by many because of funeral service and participation in community life. Since there are few secrets in small towns, most people know whether the funeral director is trustworthy or not. But there are times when even honest small-town funeral directors reap distrust of the profession. We're grateful when our services help rebuild trust, as in the following letter:

> *Thank you for your many kindnesses while handling the funeral arrangements for my father … I have had business dealings with funeral directors for many years … and I have learned to resent the sort of "plastic" people in your business, who all look the same, act the same, and mouth the same words. I also resent the sales pressures which some apply.*
>
> *My mother, my wife and I, and my kids all felt that you folks were terrific! It was a good lesson for all of us: that small town does not necessarily mean "hokey."*
>
> *While providing us with the warmth and friendliness of a small-town business, your handling of arrangements and your embalming work were exemplary and a credit to your profession!*
>
> *Thanks again!*

Funeral directors and families can work best together when families have discussed their wishes, gathered the necessary information, and made financial preparations. Planning ahead can enrich family relationships and ease stress at the time of loss.

Afterthoughts

1. How would you go about selecting a funeral home? Make a list of your available choices and begin to ask people you know about them.

2. What can families do to prepare for a conference with the funeral director?

3. Review the forms in Appendix C and D. Then list your answers (and your spouse's, if applicable) to these questions. Put these in a file with your will and other important documents, and make sure your executor or next-of-kin knows about them.

"How does one work with the clergy?"

Praise be to … the God of all comfort,
who comforts us in all our troubles,
so that we can comfort those in any trouble
with the comfort we ourselves have received from God.

II Corinthians 1:3–4

Although the person who officiates at a funeral or memorial service does not need to be ordained or "a member of the cloth," ministers, pastors, priests, rabbis, imams, chaplains, and others are often chosen by the family to officiate. Some families have relatives or friends who are clergy or seasoned public speakers. Funeral homes may have celebrants—women and men specially trained to officiate at funerals and memorial services.

Some of the tasks of the one who officiates may be to:

Provide comfort
Honor the life of the one who has died
Tell the loved one's life story
Weave that story with the sacred story
Glean wisdom that may enrich the listeners
    and community
Give thanks to God who gave life and wisdom

Commend/commit the body to earth,
   the spirit to God
Offer thanks over a meal to be shared
Provide the ministry of the Presence
Offer care beyond the service, or refer the family
   to a support group

I began officiating while I was in seminary training. A family wanted someone who wasn't the pastor of a particular church to officiate since many of their family were not churchgoers. Some family members had previously attended funerals at which ministers chided those who were not members of the flock. The family felt that was inappropriate. So, at this family's request, I gave a simple message based on the Good Shepherd of the Twenty-third Psalm and John 10.

Many times since that first service I have been asked to officiate at similar ones. As I work with people of varied faith backgrounds, I admire those who have taken responsibility for their own growth in faith. While some may grow best within religious systems or disciplines, others may need freedom from such systems.

Most funeral and memorial services are ecumenical gatherings. Some who attend are from various churches and some may not have church affiliations. Many biblical themes lend themselves well to such gatherings. The Bible's central theme, like that of all the earth's major religions, is the Golden Rule (Matthew 7:12, NRSV): "In everything do to others as you would have them do to you; for this is the law and the prophets." The Lord's Prayer (Matthew 6:9–13) is a summary of all Scripture and a pattern for peace on earth. Throughout the Bible, God is most often pictured as the Good Shepherd, which explains the popularity of Psalm 23. The Psalms have been a source of hope, comfort, and encouragement for thousands of years.

The Scripture and readings are often chosen during a meeting of the family with the person who is officiating. During this meeting a service is planned which may:

1. Remember and celebrate the life of someone who has lived and died
2. Facilitate worship that honors the loved one's faith and includes everyone
3. Give thanks to God for the gift of the loved one
4. Give thanks for the gifts she or he has brought to family and community
5. Remember and reflect on his or her unique wisdom
6. Weave this wisdom into the gathered community
7. Offer comfort, hope, and encouragement
8. Offer prayers of forgiveness, reconciliation, and healing

The family-clergy conference may include a "circle of remembrance" in which each family member is invited to share memories during the meeting. There may be questions about the mechanics of the service, such as:

1. How long would you like the service to be?
2. What Scripture would you like read?
3. Would a family member or friend like to read Scripture?
4. What Scripture would you like the message or homily based on?
5. Are there readings, poetry, or stories you would like included?
6. Would a friend or family member like to read these?
7. Will there be special music or group singing?
8. Will a close friend or family member be delivering a eulogy?

9. Will there be an open invitation for those attending
   the service to speak about the deceased?
10. Will there be a committal at the funeral home,
    church, or cemetery?
11. Will there be a nursery?
12. Will the service be followed by a luncheon?
    Who will announce this?

To assist a clergy person in preparing a eulogy or homily,
the family may be asked:

1. Describe the loved one's early childhood and
   life experiences.
2. Did he or she serve in the military? Go to college?
3. What were her or his life's work or career choices?
4. Where did he or she travel?
5. What activities and organizations were important?
6. What were the most difficult times of her or his life?
7. How did he or she cope with these?
8. What words or phrases best describe the loved one?
9. What were her or his favorite sayings?
10. Did he or she have favorite poetry (or hymns which
    may be read as poetry)?
11. Would family members like to write a letter to
    the loved one—and read it, or give permission
    for someone else to read?
12. Are there personal effects that may be used as
    visible reminders, such as crutches, a cane or
    favorite hat, something the individual made
    or cherished?
13. Are there stories that are typical of the loved
    one's life? Humorous stories?
14. What important advice did the loved one give?
15. What did she or he teach by example?

Both the eulogy and homily are shaped by Scripture and themes suggested by the family. It has been said that each person writes a book, chapter by chapter, in the living of their lives. The homily or eulogy is the epilogue of that book, written by family and friends, assisted by the one who officiates. The epilogue condenses the wisdom of a person's life, making it more memorable and useful. An epilogue is something that cannot be fully written in advance—because "we understand our lives backwards."

As I have met with families and officiated at funerals and memorial services, I have learned from each experience. One of my more memorable teachers was Hazel, a 104-year-old lady. To assist me in preparing for her service, her family gave me a letter she had once written regarding her life:

> *I remember my father, my brothers and my sister standing with me and weeping at my mother's grave. My aunt then urged my father to take me and my sister and two brothers to an orphanage so we would get proper care. My father cried when he left us there. I was healthy and spunky, but my sister had always been sickly and had sat on my mother's lap for most of her five years. She was distraught at my mother's death and being left at the orphanage.*
>
> *When I was sixteen, I left the orphanage and stayed with my aunt, uncle, and family. I was treated like a hired hand. My aunt took all of every paycheck when I worked outside the home. She promised that my needs would be met, but when I asked for clothing she gave me my cousins' discarded clothes. My father bought shoes for me because I was hard on shoes. He also took me to the movies, and he knew I was unhappy.*
>
> *After a year and a half, I left my aunt's home. I was homeless, so I asked neighbors to take me in until I could find*

a job. My first job was at a chair company. Here I learned how I had been sheltered and protected in the orphanage. The other girls who worked at the factory smoked, swore, and told dirty jokes. I quit after one week and didn't go back to pick up my paycheck. The factory was located near the railroad where hobos and drunks hung out. One girl was found murdered between the tracks.

I looked for jobs that provided room and board—there were many factories that had boarding houses. I found a job in housekeeping at a hotel where I lived with other girls in a dorm. Our meals were provided, the food was good, and there were laundry facilities. The dorm area was on the top floor of a tall building. One day one of the girls suggested we all jump off the building. I thought she was nutty. I told the main housekeeper who laughed. But I was scared and quit.

The next job I had was at a hospital where I was a waitress in the employee cafeteria and later cleaned up after the dietitian. That's where I learned safe handling of food.

I worked as a cashier in a butcher shop. Here I learned a lot about meat! I also noticed that my boss often put his finger on the scale with the meat, and that was wrong of him. I learned why one end of round steak is cut off. The most tender part is used to make cube steak, which brings a bigger price. There were all sorts of tricks of the trade.

Soon I got a job at a new hospital and was a waitress in the nurses' and doctors' dining area. I liked this job because I learned a lot by working with well educated people. I learned from my sister and other workers also. My sister had a quality many well educated people lack: wisdom.

Each change of jobs was a stepping-stone to better things. I learned something from each job, and in this way I educated myself.

When the wisdom of someone's life is shared and woven into the hearts of the listeners, the service moves quite naturally toward thanksgiving and ends on a note of victory—that death cannot take away the love or wisdom or uniqueness of anyone's life. Death cannot take away eternal life. This knowledge offers hope and comfort, which may be affirmed by a shared meal, as are many important events of life. I see the luncheon as a form of Holy Communion, which was instituted in the midst of betrayal and death. Eating together reaffirms life and well-being.

Attending and participating in many funerals has given me—as Hazel's work gave her—an education no university could provide. Wisdom gleaned from attending or officiating at funerals has helped me heal from my own accumulated grief experiences, given me new resolve for the living of my life, and helped me prepare for the time I will pass through death to new life beyond.

Afterthoughts

1. Tell your own life story in the form of a letter.

2. Write your own obituary.

3. What seems to be the theme of your life?

4.　What are your core beliefs?

5. What are your assumptions about life?

6. What are your expectations of life? Yourself? Others?

7.　How do you cope with adversity?

8.　What Scripture, music, or poetry reflects your life's journey? (These may change over time)

What are Some Ways to Celebrate Life?

*Forgetfulness leads to exile, while remembrance
is the secret of redemption.*

A sign at Yad Vashem
Holocaust Museum & Memorial
Jerusalem, Israel

Funerals—celebrations of life—bring people together to hear stories woven with poetry, songs, Scripture, flowers, and memorabilia that celebrate the life themes, significance, and wisdom of someone who has lived and died. In the weaving process, lives intersect and are transformed.

Edmund's funeral was one that offered a unique life perspective. As a young man Edmund had been drafted into military service, straight from the family farm. He was shipped across the Atlantic into the European theater of World War II. On board the ship, Edmund was amazed at the height and depth of the ocean waves. He wondered if the ship would capsize and he would sink to a watery grave. He was seasick. When he was able to eat, he sat at a long table hanging onto his plate with one hand so it wouldn't slide away as the ship rocked and tossed. He took out the pocket Bible that his church had given him and read the stories of Jesus calming stormy seas. Years later, at his funeral, Edmund's trip across the ocean became symbolic of his life's journey and was reflected in his favorite hymn:

Jesus, Saviour, Pilot Me[1]

Jesus, Saviour, pilot me
Over life's tempestuous sea:
Unknown waves before me roll,
Hiding rock and treacherous shoal;
Chart and compass come from Thee,
Jesus, Saviour, pilot me.

As a mother stills her child,
Thou canst hush the ocean wild;
Boisterous waves obey Thy will
When Thou sayest to them "Be still!"
Wondrous Sovereign of the sea,
Jesus, Saviour, pilot me.

When at last I near the shore,
And the fearful breakers roar
'Twixt me and the peaceful rest,
Then, while leaning on Thy breast,
May I hear Thee say to me,
"Fear not, I will pilot thee."

Like Edmund, Dorothea also went from a farm to serve her country overseas during World War II. During the daytime, work took her mind off her homesickness; but the nights in the barracks were long, lonely, and dark. Dorothea longed for the first light of day when activities began. Even after she returned home and lived on a farm, dawn remained her favorite time of day. At her funeral, Dorothea's love of dawn was made memorable as everyone sang her favorite hymn, "When Morning Gilds the Skies."

Sometimes family members write original poems or compose songs to celebrate a loved one's life, much the way biblical psalms and laments were composed and sung upon the death of a leader. Whether the song is an original composition, a recorded song that resonates with someone's life, or a traditional song or hymn, nearly everyone has a favorite that may reflect a life theme. All-time favorite hymns often create word pictures that tell the story of faith, such as: "In the Garden," "The Old Rugged Cross," "Rock of Ages," "Savior, Like a Shepherd Lead Us."

Sometimes poetry such as the Psalms reflects the theme of someone's life. Millie was a country girl who served overseas during World War II. Far away from home and family, Millie coped with her strange new environment by memorizing Psalm 46 and meditating on it: "God is our refuge and strength, a very present help in trouble. Therefore will not we fear, though the earth be removed, and though the mountains be carried into the midst of the sea ... Be still, and know that I am God." (Psalm 46:1–2, 10a KJV) The wisdom of this psalm continued to guide her through the challenges of marriage and family as well as life as a widow and single parent. Psalm 46 took on new life when it became the theme of her funeral service.

Lorraine didn't serve in the military, but there were other hardships. She grew up on a farm, milking cows and working in the fields. When she was fourteen, her father died suddenly. Her mother sent her to a large city to work and send money to help her family. This was in a time when there were no governmental programs for widows and orphans. In her strange new surroundings far from home, Lorraine adopted Psalm 27 as her theme: "The Lord is my light and my salvation; whom shall I fear? The Lord is the strength of my life; of whom shall I be afraid?" (Psalm 27:1, KJV) Many years later at Lorraine's funeral, a female vocalist sang Psalm 27 in clear ringing tones, which echoed in the hearts of the hearers long after the service.

Besides poetry, songs, and psalms, a person's life journey may be woven with historical figures or events. Harold, another World War II veteran, was trained as a mechanic and driver, then shipped overseas. He did his job with such distinction that he eventually became a driver for General George S. Patton, Jr.. Harold kept his brush with fame quite private. But when he died his family celebrated this honor by displaying a framed commendation signed by the famous general.

An act of faith or generosity may also become the theme of someone's life. Marjorie never spoke a word about her faith, never attended church, never told anyone, even her children, about a favorite Scripture or song. But whenever a relative, friend, neighbor, or acquaintance had an illness or loss, Marjorie brought over her famous stew and biscuits. Her life reflected the theme of one of Jesus's parables: "Just as you did it to one of the least of these who are members of my family, you did it to me." (Matthew 25:40 NRSV)

One family's act of generosity was done so secretly that no one in their small church or community knew about it. Only after both the Linwoods had died did their children reveal their generous gift to the church's building project. The gift was so large in proportion to their income that they were audited by the IRS for that year. The Linwoods' quiet generosity was an inspiration to many.

Sometimes a tool one uses daily may become symbolic of his or her life's journey. Barney had a debilitating bone disease and had difficulty walking. In his later years he could only walk by using crutches. In time, Barney found other creative uses for his crutches. He used them as remote controls for the television, before digital remotes. He used the crutches to reach objects beyond arm's length, to prod his children into doing their homework and household tasks, or to click together to get someone's attention. Even after he was confined to a wheelchair, Barney continued his creative use of crutches, which became the subject of family jokes. At Barney's funeral, the pastor held up Barney's crutches and told some of these stories. He then mused about what Barney's new life might be like, imagining Barney leaping and dancing, no longer needing crutches.

Sometimes a loved one's handmade items become symbolic of their life. Audra could sew, do upholstery, knit, crochet, cross-stitch and embroider. She often gave handmade gifts to her family and friends. She knitted a brown face mask for John that extended beneath his jacket to keep his head and neck warm while he was clearing snow. When she heard I was going to Israel, she made me a small blue mesh case for my earrings. While John cleared snow and I traveled, we each had reminders of Audra's thoughtfulness. Several years later, when I officiated at her service, I held up the brown mask and blue earring case as examples of Audra's resourcefulness, generosity, and thoughtfulness, much like that of the biblical Dorcas.

Throughout the world, rites of death involve care of the physical body—embalming, mummification, burial, or burning—aiding the soul in making a transition from the "land of the living" to its "final resting place," and reordering social relationships disrupted by death. In many cultures, to be a dead member of one's society is the individual's ultimate social status.

As a learned Christian friend pointed out to me, after years of sad and somber funerals, it dawned on Christians to sound the note of triumph and victory like Paul did: "O Death, where is thy sting? O grave, where is thy victory? ...

But thanks be to God, which giveth us the victory through our Lord Jesus Christ" (I Corinthians 15:55, 57 KJV). Faith enables Christians to become a bit more impudent and in-your-face in response to death, having a service of praise and thanksgiving, and making the luncheon afterwards a grand party.[2]

While victory over death and assurance of eternal life are part of most funeral services, not everyone may be able to move to the Hallelujah Chorus in an hour's time. If a death has been sudden, there may be shock and numbness, difficulty concentrating, eating, sleeping, and performing daily tasks. If there has been a long bedside vigil, there may be exhaustion. There may be unresolved issues. Healing may come through being together for the visitation and funeral, through shared stories, tears, and laughter, through the melodies and rhythms of music, through the beauty of floral arrangements. Deep peace may come as family and friends simply sit quietly together.

Remembering and giving thanks for the gift of life can open the heart to receive comfort, peace, and joy. In the valley of the shadow of death, the soul can be restored.

The funeral service celebrates life, weaving wisdom from one life into the lives of many in a way that builds and enriches community. As the community remembers, celebrates, and receives these gifts, the life of someone who has died can go on speaking.

Through my years of participation in funeral service, I've learned wisdom and faith I may not have found anywhere else. Poetry, music, Scripture, history, and ordinary household items have taken on new meaning because they've been the theme of someone's life. As I live and work in a funeral home, I continue to experience transformation and change.

I often wonder about the women who came to care for

Jesus's body after his execution. If they had avoided their ritual of caring for the body, would they also have missed the blessing of becoming the first witnesses of the resurrection, the pinnacle of the Christian faith? If I had avoided participating in funeral service because of my grief baggage, would I too have missed the blessings that these celebrations of life offer?

Although attending funerals isn't easy, the gift of presence is an act of courage and faith; for in the intersection between life and death, individuals, families, and communities are changed, transformed, and blessed.

Afterthoughts

1. Is life a *right* or a *gift*?

2. What meaning do rituals and traditions have for you? (*Refer to Appendix H-2 for a list of biblical customs and traditions.*)

3. How might celebrations of life play a part in the transformation of individuals? Families? Communities?

4. Begin to jot notes about your favorite Scripture, hymns, and funeral rituals that you might like to be celebrated for you. Keep this list with other important papers. Let someone know about your preferences.

HOW DOES ONE GO ON LIVING
AFTER A LOVED ONE HAS DIED?

Love never ends ...

I Corinthians 13:8a, NRSV

"Keeping busy.""Taking one minute, one hour, one day at a
time." "Remembering." "Talking." "Crying." "Walking."
"Working in my garden." "Scrubbing floors on my hands
and knees." "Going golfing." "Cleaning closets and drawers."
"Walking my dog.""Boiling something.""Taking naps."

These are some answers that people give in response to
the question posed by this chapter's title. Coping mechanisms
and time frames may be different for each person and each
grief experience. While some may prefer being active, others may listen to music or take a quiet walk in nature. While
some may run from grief or fight against it, others may approach it with curiosity—like a mysterious gift in crumpled
brown paper wrapping.

Grief is the human response to loss, a process of moving from orientation, through disorientation, to reorientation.
Grief is a necessary part of human growth and transformation,
and each loss is followed by gain. Anticipating a positive out-

come can help in moving through the grief process. Grief is an energy that can be put to good use, as Tom discovered.

Grief is an Energy

Tom was young, married just three years, working as a plant custodian. After work he often ran five miles along the country roads near his home to stay in shape. But after his wife died suddenly, Tom felt a need to "pound things." Since his friends were in the midst of a do-it-yourself addition to their home, Tom volunteered his help. Through vigorous physical activity, he released much of his frustration and grief, gave his friends some much-needed help, and enjoyed the new addition with his friends until a new love came into his life. Like many before him, Tom discovered that grief is an energy that can be used in constructive ways. While the gray matter of the brain contains small muscles that can be easily burned out by grief, the body's larger muscles are well designed to discharge grief energy.

Grief Brings Bodily Changes

Grief brings many changes to the body. There may be muscle tightness in the back, throat, or chest; headaches; difficulty concentrating; increased anxiety, panic attacks, stomach upsets, sleep disturbances, and fatigue. Sometimes grief masquerades as low blood sugar. Fruit, fruit juice, or other nutritious snacks between regular meals may be helpful.

Selfcare—eating healthy foods, getting adequate rest and exercise—is especially important. Tending one's grief is important because grief that is turned inward, ignored, sidetracked or not fully processed can complicate daily life and interfere with the natural healing process.

Moving on Too Soon

When Ward's wife Kate was killed in a car accident, leaving him with two young children, Ward was overwhelmed with grief. He blamed himself for not driving Kate that day, for letting her drive a compact car while he drove a pickup, for not going to the grocery store himself. Besides the shock and numbness of grief, Ward discovered he was poorly prepared to manage a household, care for the children, handle finances, prepare meals, do laundry, clean, and so on. Soon he was deep in debt. He said, "I didn't realize how much Kate's home-making skills contributed to our family's standard of living until I took the kids shopping for school clothes. I got sticker shock."

Overwhelmed by the demands at home and work along with his grief, Ward began dating Erica, a widow with a young child, hoping this diversion would relieve his loneliness and help him get on with his life. Fifteen months after Kate's death, Ward and Erica were married. She and her son moved in with Ward and his children. While it seemed like a storybook solution for a widower and widow, the harsh reality was quite different. Erica's and Ward's children did not get along. Ward's daughter moved away to live with relatives. His son was arrested for underage drinking. In counseling, Ward and Erica discovered they were still grieving their first spouses, and their home life probably wouldn't improve until they each tended their inner wounds.

While counseling was helpful to Ward and Erica, the process took time, and some tensions remained. A few years later

Ward had a heart attack, and Erica was diagnosed with breast cancer. They learned what healthcare professionals have long suspected: Unprocessed grief can be an underlying cause of many illnesses and physical conditions. Ward and Erica again focused on self care: adequate rest, exercise, relaxation, nourishing food, self-chosen social lives.

A Costly Side Trip

Like Ward, Cara also took a side trip from the painful early months of her grief. Cara's husband Marc had a heart attack at work and died on the way to the hospital. There was no time for her and their four children to say goodbye. They went through the funeral in shock and grief. In the weeks that followed they were in varying stages of anger, denial, and "if only's," each grieving in different ways at different times.

A few months after the funeral, Dan, an old high school flame, contacted Cara. He was recently divorced and looking for companionship. He took her to restaurants, out dancing, to movies, shopping, and on weekend getaways. Cara found Dan's attention a welcome relief from her loneliness and grief.

But while Cara was enjoying her fling, her children got into trouble at school, and she made frequent trips to the principal's office. After a few months Dan took a job in Phoenix, and the romance cooled. But the damage remained. Another loss had been added to Cara's initial grief. In the meantime, Cara's early support from family and friends eroded, and she was left to deal with troubled children in addition to her own grief. Cara's sidetrip from grief was costly. It took a long time to sort through an interrupted grief process and reweave the family system.

An Unpaid Job

The loss of a loved one presents survivors with many tasks in addition to already busy lives. There are financial and legal matters to tend, changes in real estate and vehicle titles, and other personal property decisions to make. Each change and detail is a reminder that the death of a loved one forever changes the lives of survivors. While these tasks may seem overwhelming at first, one usually does not have to do them alone. Family, friends, and neighbors offer help. Survivors can often choose which tasks they wish to do themselves and which to delegate.

The death of a loved one also changes family gatherings and holiday celebrations. Friendships, too, may change. Some may come closer while others distance themselves. Consideration and respect for the ways others grieve and care for themselves is helpful in maintaining friendships.

Knowing what to expect from the grief process can also be helpful. Fortunately, some who have traveled "the valley of the shadow of death" and studied the grief process have made maps for those who follow. One of the early mapmakers was Elisabeth Kubler-Ross, who identified five landmarks, or stages, of grief: denial, anger, bargaining, depression, and acceptance.[1]

Another is Granger E. Westberg, who identified the following ten stages:

1. *We are in a state of shock*
2. *We express emotion*
3. *We feel depressed and very lonely*
4. *We may experience physical symptoms of distress*
5. *We may become panicky*
6. *We feel a sense of guilt about the loss*

7. *We are filled with anger and resentment*
8. *We resist returning*
9. *Gradually hope comes through*
10. *We struggle to affirm reality*[2]

Survivors may not experience all these stages; and, if they do, it may not be in any particular order or time frame. Even so, an occasional glance at a map may be helpful while also paying attention to one's own needs and making one's own discoveries. The loss will always be there, but, with support, the loose strands can be creatively rewoven in a way that enriches individuals, families, and communities.

Meanwhile, selfcare includes looking out for one's own welfare. This may seem "selfish" at first, but one cannot love others as much as oneself if one does not first love and take care of oneself. Grieving people often receive advice—sometimes well intended, sometimes self serving—to sell their home, move in with grown children or friends, travel, donate to charities. However, the loss of a loved one is a big enough change; if possible, it's best not to make other major changes—at least during the first year. Survivors have the power to buy time and save integrity by saying, "I'll think about it." For major decisions that need to be made sooner, one can do research and seek wisdom from reliable sources outside the circle of family and friends.

There are many resources available for survivors. These include support groups, books, tapes, and videos, and some of these are listed in Appendix I. Some of my favorites are *How To Survive the Loss of a Love*[3] and the Abbey Press *CareNotes*[4] series because they are easy to read and offer helpful information and further resources. *CareNotes* can often be found in hospitals, hospices, churches, and funeral homes.

To condense the many books and articles I've read and seminars I've attended, I offer two lists, one of more active methods and one more contemplative.

Active methods of grieving:

Cry it out (Alone or with someone).

Talk it out (Alone, with a picture, with God, with a friend, in a tape recorder).

Laugh it out (Yes, a good laugh is as healing as a good cry).

Work it out (Keep hands busy).

Exercise it out (Body movement).

Walk it out (Use the body's big muscles).

Play it out (Children and pets can help).

Scream it out (A car can make a good scream chamber).

Breathe it out (Blowing up balloons).

Bathe or shower it out (Water therapy).

Swim it out (More water therapy).

Massage it out (And making use of other healing arts).

Sing it out (It may be the beginning of a new career!).

Do something kind for someone else (Perhaps in secret, expecting nothing in return).

Contemplative methods of grieving:

Do nothing, just *be* (as dogs and cats illustrate).

Pamper oneself

Write (There may be a budding poet within; if not, it can be shredded later).

Have a conversation with the deceased loved one, God, or Grief-as-Teacher.

Watch a movie that makes you cry or laugh—
get it out vicariously.
Take up photography—find beauty in
unexpected places.
Learn something new—go to the library.
Take a class in yoga or painting.
Make one small change—rearrange one
thing in the home, vary one's morning
or evening routine.
Stitch, quilt, knit, crochet, or other arts and crafts
Ask again, "Why am I here?"
Watch the clouds, wonder about the
"cloud of witnesses" (Hebrews 12:1).
Stargaze (stars are always present but can only
be seen at night).
Read psalms which have comforted people
for thousands of years.
Read the stories of Jesus, put oneself into
the story and have a conversation with Jesus
or someone in the story.
Attend a grief support group (funeral homes, hospice,
hospitals, churches, schools, and libraries).

Caution should be taken regarding sharing in groups or on the Internet. Grief can make one particularly vulnerable, and there is no shortage of opportunists! In Western culture, some think the grieving process takes about two weeks (although two years would be more realistic). Some widows and widowers have received romantic offers within two weeks of their loss. Caution is also in order regarding alcohol, caffeine, and other substances that may seem to offer temporary relief but which actually work against the grief process.

Another Kind of Grief

While much of this chapter has focused on moving forward *after* a loss, there is another kind of grief—anticipatory grief—when a loss is imminent. Some families have creative ways of celebrating life and love in the midst of illness and approaching death.

One family with a child dying of cancer held a party at their church, celebrating life—because little Carter always loved parties!

Some families gather around their dying loved ones and sing the great hymns of the faith.

Veronica, a young mother dying of kidney disease, wanted to prepare her 5-year-old daughter Marissa for her approaching death. As she lay in her bed, Veronica sang and taught Marissa psalms and hymns of the faith that have sustained people for many years. Veronica creatively shaped Marissa's faith, giving her music, words, and phrases to help her go on after the loss of her mother.

Hymns can offer comfort and hope to those who are facing loss, as the words from the following hymns do:

> *Ye fearful saints, fresh courage take*
> *The clouds ye so much dread*
> *Are big with mercy and will break*
> *In blessings on your head* [5]

> "God Moves in a Mysterious Way"
> William Cowper

> *In suff'ring love the thread of life*
> *Is woven thro' our care,*
> *For God is with us, not alone*
> *Our pain and toil we bear.*

In love's deep womb our fears are held;
There God's rich tears are sown
And bring to birth, in hope new-born,
The strength to journey on.

In suff'ring love our God comes now,
Hope's vision born in gloom;
With tears and laughter shared and blessed
The desert yet will bloom.[6]

"In Suffering Love"
Rob Johns and Elinor F. Johns

While I was writing this chapter, I read the story of Katie, a 21-year-old woman dying of cancer, who mustered all her remaining strength, put on a wedding gown, left her oxygen tank and wheelchair at the back of the church, and walked down the aisle to marry her sweetheart, Nick. Four hundred guests attended the ceremony and reception. It was the happiest day of Katie's life, and she was radiant.

Five days later, Katie died. Some 1,200 people attended her funeral. On the program were printed words Katie had written for a speech at her high school graduation: "Life is a fragile chain of experiences held together by love. If there could be only one thing in life to learn, it would be to love.

"If only you can love enough, you will be the happiest and most powerful person in the world."

Katie knew love's powerful and eternal nature. So even in the presence of illness and death, she celebrated life and love.[7]

"And now faith, hope, and love abide, these three; and the greatest of these is love." (I Corinthians 13:13, NRSV)

Afterthoughts

1. Are people *human beings* or *human doings*?

2. Why can one celebrate life and love in the midst of illness and dying?

3. How have you responded to your own grief in the past? What have you learned in order to deal with any grief yet to come?

Appendix A

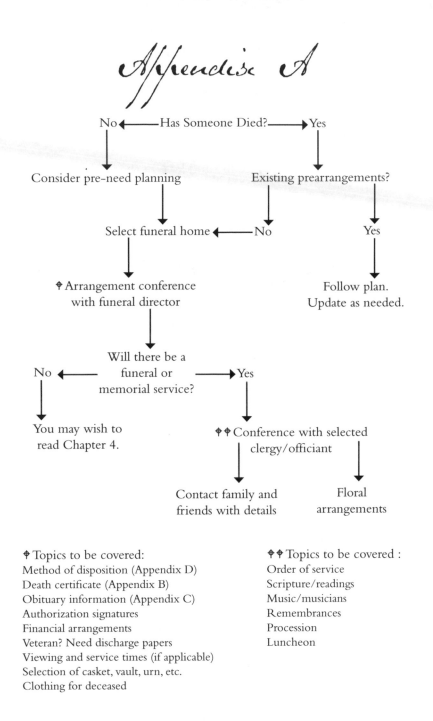

No ◄——— Has Someone Died? ———► Yes

Consider pre-need planning　　　　　Existing prearrangements?

Select funeral home ◄——— No　　　　　　　Yes

✝ Arrangement conference　　　　　　Follow plan.
with funeral director　　　　　　Update as needed.

No ◄——— Will there be a
funeral or ———► Yes
memorial service?

You may wish to
read Chapter 4.

✝✝ Conference with selected
clergy/officiant

Contact family and　　　　　Floral
friends with details　　　arrangements

✝ Topics to be covered:
Method of disposition (Appendix D)
Death certificate (Appendix B)
Obituary information (Appendix C)
Authorization signatures
Financial arrangements
Veteran? Need discharge papers
Viewing and service times (if applicable)
Selection of casket, vault, urn, etc.
Clothing for deceased

✝✝ Topics to be covered :
Order of service
Scripture/readings
Music/musicians
Remembrances
Procession
Luncheon

Appendix B

DEATH CERTIFICATE INFORMATION

The following information is needed for a Certificate of Death.
Note: Each state requires information about the decedent—
the following is taken from a Michigan certificate—other
states may vary but most of the information is needed. Check
with your local county to see which information is required
in your state.

You may find it helpful to copy these and other pages in
the appendices and fill in the information to help with your
funeral plans. We give you permission and encourage you to
do so.

Decedent's name
_____
First, Middle, Last

Date of birth
_____
Month, Day, Year

Sex
_____

Date of death
_____
Month, Day, Year

Name at birth or other name used for personal business
Include aliases, if any.

_____

_____

Age
_____
Last birthday, in years.

Location of death
_____
Place where deceased was officially pronounced dead, including city, village or township of death, and county of death.

Current residence
_____
Street address, county, city, village or township, and zip code

Birthplace
_____
City and state

Social Security number
_____

Decedent's education
_____
Highest degree or level of school completed.

Race
_____
American Indian, Caucasian, African-American, etc.
If Asian, give nationality; i.e., Chinese, Filipino, Asian Indian, etc.

Ancestry
_____
Mexican, Cuban, Arab, African, English, French, Dutch, etc.
If American Indian race, enter principal tribe.

Was decedent ever in U.S. Armed Forces?
_____

Usual occupation
_____

Kind of business or industry
_____

Marital status
_____

Name of surviving spouse
_____
If wife, give name before first married.

Father's name
_____
First, Middle, Last

Mother's name before first married
_____
First, Middle, Last

Informant's name
_____
Relationship to decedent and address

Method of disposition
_____
Burial, cremation, entombment, donation, removal, storage

Place of disposition
_____
Name of cemetery, crematory, or other location.

Location of disposition
_____
Address of above-named

The remainder of the items are to be completed by the certifying physician and registrar. There are two remaining items which may be asked of family:

Did tobacco use contribute to the death?
Yes, No, Probably, or Unknown
(Medical Examiners tell us if a person smoked "Yes" must be circled.)

If Female
Pregnant within past year; pregnant at time of death; not pregnant, but pregnant within 42 days of death; not pregnant, but pregnant 43 days to 1 year before death; unknown if pregnant within the past year.

You will need Death Certificates for the following:
Real estate (one for each property description), vehicles, bank accounts, stocks, bonds, insurance, IRS, veterans benefits, etc.

Appendix C

OBITUARY INFORMATION

This is information that is helpful in the writing of an obituary. Some families choose to write the obituary themselves. Others provide obituary information to the funeral home or local newspaper so they can write the obituary for them.

Decedent's name
_____

Age
_____

Date of death
_____

Location of death
_____

Date of birth
_____

Place of birth
_____

Names of parents (including mother's maiden name)
_____

Marriage date
_____

Spouse's name
_____

Place of marriage
_____

Military service
_____

Education
_____

Employment _____

Affiliations _____

Hobbies/interests _____

Survivors (*Spouse, children, grandchildren, great-grandchildren, mother/ father, sisters/brothers, special friends.*)

_____

_____

_____

_____

Preceded in death by _____

Day and date of service _____

Time of service _____

Location of service _____

Name of person officiating _____

Time and location of visitation or wake _____

Time of rosary/prayer or lodge service, if any _____

_____

Memorial contributions _____

(Optional photo)

Appendix D

METHODS OF DISPOSITION

This may be based on the wishes of the deceased and/or the needs of close family members at the time death occurs.

The Michigan death certificate lists three choices (other states may vary):

Burial

A. Following embalming, viewing, and service with body present (most cemeteries require the use of a vault or outer burial container)

B. Direct burial with or without embalming—(Michigan state law requires that burial must take place within forty-eight hours of death without embalming but other states may vary)

C. Green burial—back-to-nature burials in biodegradable caskets, available in some areas. Check out more information at www.memorialecosystems.com

D. Family-owned cemeteries (these usually require prior arrangements with local government)

Cremation

A. Following embalming, viewing and service with body present

B. Following private viewing at place of death or funeral home

C. Direct—without viewing or service with body present

Donation

A. To a medical or educational institution (requires prior arrangements with facility)

Appendix E

GENERAL/ITEMIZED PRICE LIST

The following is a sample price list. All funeral providers are required by law (which varies by state) to provide pricing information. Ask for an itemized list from your local funeral director. Most reputable funeral homes provide this information without being asked.

GENERAL PRICE LIST

These prices are effective as of: _____

This general price list is provided in compliance with Federal Trade Commission Regulations governing funeral homes. You may retain it for your records.

The goods and services shown below are those we can provide to our clients. You may choose only the items you desire. However, any funeral arrangements you select will include a charge for our basic services and overhead. If legal or other requirements mean you must buy any items you did not specifically ask for, we will explain the reason in writing on the statement we provide describing the funeral goods and services you selected.

There are other items that you need to purchase, such as, cemetery or crematory services, newspaper notices, markers, final date lettering. These items will not appear on the statement of funeral goods and services you selected. These cash items must be paid before the day of services.

ITEMIZED SELECTIONS

Basic service of funeral director and staff $ _____

Our fee for the basic service of funeral director and staff includes, but is not limited to: staff to respond to initial request for service, arrangement conference with family or responsible parties, arrangement of funeral, preparation and filing of necessary authorizations and permits, recording vital statistics, preparation and placement of obituary notice, and coordination with those providing other portions of the funeral, e.g., cemetery, crematory, vault companies, and others as required. Also included in this charge are overhead expenses relative to our facilities such as professional licensing, legal and accounting fees, insurance, building and utility expenses, parking lot and grounds, maintenance, taxes, equipment, furnishings, inventory costs, recordkeeping, and secretarial and administrative expenses.

This fee for our basic services and overhead will be added to the total cost of the funeral arrangements you select. This is a **non-declinable item**. (This fee is already included in our charges for direct cremations, immediate burials, and forwarding or receiving of remains.)

PREPARATION AND CARE OF REMAINS

Standard and autopsy embalming $ _____

Except in certain special cases, embalming is not required by law. Michigan law requires embalming when death was caused by certain infectious diseases or, with very limited exceptions, when the body is not taken to its final destination such as cemetery or certain funeral arrangements, such as a funeral with viewing. If you do not want embalming, you usually have the right to choose an arrangement that does not require you to pay for it, such as direct cremation or immediate burial.

Other preparation of body $ _____

This charge includes dressing of remains, cosmetology, washing and thorough disinfection and manicuring

USE OF FACILITIES AND STAFF AND EQUIPMENT FOR VIEWING

This charge is for our facility and staff for viewing, visitation, wake, family hour, per day, or any portion thereof

Visitation/Viewing (Conducted at Funeral Home) per day
$ _____

Visitation/Viewing (Conducted at another facility) per day
$ _____

USE OF FACILITIES AND STAFF AND EQUIPMENT FOR FUNERAL SERVICES

Funeral Ceremony (Conducted at Funeral Home)
$ _____

Funeral Ceremony (Conducted at another facility)
$ _____

Memorial Service (Conducted at Funeral Home)
$ _____

Memorial Service (Conducted at another facility)
$ _____

Graveside Services $ _____

Transfer of remains to funeral home (Within thirty-five miles of service area) $ _____

Hearse or custom funeral vehicle (Within thirty-five miles of service area) $ _____

The charge for additional miles is $ _____ per one-way mile

TRANSPORTATION

Transportation outside of local service area per one-way mile
$ _____
(Local service area is thirty-five miles)

MERCHANDISE

Caskets—we offer caskets which range in prices from
$ _____ to $ _____

A complete price list will be provided at the funeral home office.

Outer burial container or grave liner—we offer outer burial containers that range in price from $ _____ to $ _____

An outer burial container is not required by Michigan Law, however most cemeteries require outer burial containers, sometimes called grave liners or concrete box. A complete price list will be provided at the funeral home office.

Memorial packages ranging in price from $ _____ to $ _____

Memorial packages include register book, memorial folders, acknowledgment cards

ALTERNATIVE PACKAGE SELECTIONS

Forwarding of remains to another funeral home
$ _____

This package includes removal of remains from local place of death, limited basic services of funeral director and staff, embalming, transfer container for remains (combination container/air tray), necessary authorizations, and arrangements with airlines or other carriers. This does not include viewing or visitation, rites or ceremonies prior to forwarding of the remains. Transfer to airport or custom carrier not included.

Receiving remains from another funeral home with no service $ _____

This charge includes basic limited services of funeral director and staff, automotive equipment, and transportation to cemetery.

Receiving of remains from another funeral home with funeral services $ _____

This charge includes receiving of remains from another funeral home; temporary shelter of remains; obtaining necessary authorizations; basic services of funeral director and staff; and facilities for visitation, wake, family hour, or any combination thereof; at church or our chapel, graveside service, and necessary automotive equipment. Transportation within thirty-five mile service area is also included.

IMMEDIATE BURIALS

Prices range from $ _____ to $ _____
Our charge for an immediate burial without any rites or ceremonies includes:
Removal charge within service area, shelter of remains, transportation to local cemetery, necessary basic services of funeral director and staff, and obtaining authorizations. Also includes use of hearse for transporting to cemetery.

1. Immediate burial with casket selected from our funeral home $ _____

2. Immediate burial with container provided by consumer $ _____

NOTE: Prior to the immediate burial, it is the policy of our funeral home to require identification of the deceased by the next of kin or other person or persons in charge of making arrangements for this type of service. The identification shall take place in the funeral home chapel at no extra charge.

CREMATION

Prices range from $ _____ to $ _____

DIRECT CREMATION

Our charge for a direct cremation includes removal of remains from place of death within service area, basic services of funeral director and staff and use of service or custom funeral vehicle. If you want to arrange a direct cremation, you can use an alternative container. Alternative containers encase the body and can be made of materials such as fiberboard or composition materials.

1. Direct cremation with casket selected from our funeral home $ _____

2. Direct cremation with alternative container (minimum, heavy cardboard) $ _____

3. Direct cremation with container provided by purchaser $ _____

NOTE: Prior to the direct cremation process, it is the policy of our funeral home to require identification of the deceased by the next of kin or other person or persons in charge of making arrangements for this type of service. The identification shall take place in the funeral home chapel at no extra charge.

URNS

A complete selection of urns will be provided for you. We have selections ranging in price from $ _____ to $ _____

We also have a selection of Urn Vaults for earth burial or Urns.
Anatomical donations $ _____

Price includes limited basic services of funeral director and staff, removal in service area, service vehicle for transportation to University, other preparation of remains, and shelter of remains. This does not include mileage to University or other facility.

CASH ADVANCE ITEMS

Cemetery Charges $ _____

Death Certificates $ _____

Crematory Charges $ _____

Musician $ _____

Clergy Honorarium $ _____

Obituary Notice $ _____

Flowers $ _____

Luncheon $ _____

Note: In addition to itemized prices, there may be "package pricing" such as "Funeral Service Package with Burial" or "Memorial Service Package with Cremation."

DISCLOSURES

These disclosures are required by and conform to the 1984 Federal Trade Commission rules and updates, related to the practice of Mortuary Science. Disclaimers of warranties and other disclosures will be given in writing as required.

TERMS

All funerals are considered a **cash transaction.** All cash outlays are to be paid at the time of the funeral, such as cemetery, clergymen, transportation, etc. If payment is not made within thirty days from time of serving family, a penalty for "unanticipated late payment" will be charged. An additional charge will be made for estates.

Appendix I

FINANCIAL METHODS AND RESOURCES

Resources for payment for funerals:

Pre-Need:
Prepayment to funeral home, trusted to third party escrow agent

Funeral or Life Insurance

At-Need:
Pre-need trust agency remits to funeral home
upon presentation of certified death certificate

Assignment of benefits on a life insurance policy

Savings

Dividing cost among family members

Social Security death benefit of $255 to surviving spouse

Veterans Benefits

Credit Card

Appendix 9

OUTLINE OF A CELEBRATION OF LIFE

The following is a sample order of service, which can be adapted for various faith traditions.

Prelude (organ, piano, ensemble, recorded)

Greetings/Introduction of Service/Invitation to Luncheon

Scripture Sentences or Poetry

Congregational Hymn or Song

Prayer

Scripture Readings (Psalm 23, John 14:1–6)

Eulogy and/or Public Sharing of Memories

Special Music

Homily or Eulogy

Prayer with The Lord's Prayer

Congregational Hymn

Committal (or announcement of committal at graveside)

Postlude (organ, piano, ensemble, recorded music)

Appendix H1

Scriptures Commonly Used at Funerals

The following list was gleaned from hundreds of funeral messages I've transcribed through the years. The most common are in bold-faced type. All are from the Holy Bible, New Revised Standard Version, unless otherwise noted.

Genesis 1:27 *Men and women were created in the image of God.*

Genesis 2:7–9, 15 *God planted a garden in Eden, created people to till and keep it.*

Genesis 5:21–24 *Enoch walked with God; God took him.*

Genesis 8:15–19 *Noah and family went out from ark to be fruitful and multiply.*

Genesis 9:9–10, 12, 16 *People and animals are included in the Noahic covenant with a rainbow as its sign.*

Genesis 12:1–3 *Covenant with Abraham—blessings to be extended to whole earth.*

Genesis 47:27–31 *Jacob's instructions to Joseph to be buried with his ancestors.*

Genesis 48:15–16 *God "shepherded" Jacob all his life long.*

Genesis 49:29–33 *Jacob repeats burial instructions and dies.*

Exodus 15:13 *Moses' song: God loved, redeemed, guided people.*

Exodus 33:12–23 *God's presence and glory shown to Moses.*

Numbers 23:10 *Balaam: "Let me die the death of the upright."*

Deuteronomy 4:7 *What nation has a God so near?*

Deuteronomy 29:29a *The secret things belong to God; revealed things to us.*

Deuteronomy 31:1–8 *Moses transfers leadership to Joshua: God will not fail or forsake.*

Deuteronomy 33:27 *Eternal God is refuge; underneath are*
everlasting arms. (KJV)

Ruth *The story of a Moabite woman who redeems*
Israelite family; David's ancestors.

II Samuel 12:15–23 *Death of David's child.*

II Samuel 14:14 *"We must all die."*

II Samuel 22:2, 3 *God is a rock, fortress, and deliverer;*
saves us from violence.

II Kings 23:1–7 *King Josiah finds and reads law, cleanses temple.*

I Chronicles 29:28 *David dies old and full of days.*

II Chronicles 7:14 *If people humble themselves, God will forgive*
and heal.

Job 1:1-3, 9, 13-22 *Righteous Job is tested.*

Job 1:21 The *Lord gave and takes away.*

Job 4:8 *Those who sow trouble reap the same.*

Job 5:17 *Happy is the one God reproves or disciplines.*

Job 7:7 *"My life is a breath."*

Job 14:1–2, 7–12, 14 *Job struggles, prays, and asks, "If mortals die,*
will they live again?"

Job 19:25–27 *"I know that my Redeemer lives."*

Job 22.21 *"Agree with God and be at peace; good will*
come to you."

Job 30:23 *"I know that you will bring me to death and to the*
house appointed for all living."

Job 42:10–17 *God restores the fortunes of Job; Job dies old*
and full of days.

Psalm 1 *Happy are the righteous; the wicked perish.*

Psalm 3:5 *"I lie down and sleep; I wake again;*
for God sustains me."

Psalm 5:3, 8 *"God hears the faithful; lead me O Lord in*
your righteousness."

Psalm 8 *"How majestic is your name in all the earth!"*

Psalm 15 *"Who may dwell on your holy hill?" Moral qualities*
of the people of God.

Psalm 16:7–8 *God gives counsel in the night; "I keep the Lord always before me" (v. 8).*

Psalm 17:15 *"I shall behold your face in righteousness."*

Psalm 18:1–2 *"I love you, O Lord, my strength …*
rock … deliverer."

Psalm 19:7–11 *The law of God revives us, makes us wise.*

Psalm 23 *"The Lord is my Shepherd"(NRSV; KJV).*
(See also John 10.)

Psalm 24:1–4 *The earth is the Lord's. Who may ascend?*

Psalm 25 *"To you, O Lord, I lift up my soul" (v. 1).*
Prayer for deliverance.

Psalm 27 *"The Lord is my light and my salvation" (v. 1).*

Psalm 28:6–7 *"Blessed be the Lord, for he has heard."*

Psalm 30:2, 5 *"I cried … for help, and you have healed me."*
Weeping at night, joy in morning.

Psalm 31 *"Into your hand I commit my spirit" (v. 5).*
Prayer for deliverance.

Psalm 33:20 *"Our soul waits for the Lord."*

Psalm 34:1–9, 15, 22 *"I will bless the Lord at all times."*

Psalm 36:7–9 *"How precious is your steadfast love." (v. 7a)*

Psalm 37 *"Do not fret because of the wicked." (v. 23–28);*
"The Lord holds us by the hand" (v. 1).

Psalm 39:4–7, 12 *"Lord, let me know my end" (v. 4);*
"Do not hold your peace at my tears" (v. 12c).

Psalm 40 *"I waited patiently for the Lord" (v. 1).*

Psalm 41:10 *"Be gracious to me and raise me up."*

Psalm 42:1–2, 11 *"As the deer longs for flowing streams" (v. 1a).*
"Why are you cast down, O my soul?" (v. 5a)

Psalm 43:3 *"O send out your light and your truth."*

Psalm 46 *"God is our refuge and strength, a very present help in trouble" (v. 1).*

Psalm 48:9 *"We ponder your steadfast love."*

Psalm 49:15 *"God will ransom my soul."*

Psalm 51 *"Have mercy on me ... wash ... cleanse ,. create in me a clean heart."*

Psalm 55:22 *"Cast your burden upon the Lord."*

Psalm 56 *"Be gracious to me, O God."*

Psalm 61:1–4 *"Lead me to the rock that is higher than I" (v. 2b).*

Psalm 62:1–2 *"For God alone my soul waits in silence" (v. 1a).*

Psalm 71:1–3–24 *God as strong refuge.*

Psalm 73:23–26 *God guides with counsel, receives with honor.*

Psalm 75:6–7 *"It is God who executes judgment" (v. 7a).*

Psalm 84:1–3, 5, 11–12 *"How lovely is your dwelling place," swallow finds nest; doorkeeper in God's house.*

Psalm 86 *"Incline your ear ... teach me ... show me a sign of your favor."*

Psalm 89:47–48 *"Remember how short my time is."*

Psalm 90:12 *"Teach us to count our days that we may gain a wise heart."*

Psalm 91 *"You who live in the shelter of the Most High ... shadow of Almighty."*

Psalm 93 *God as king who established the world; it shall never be moved.*

Psalm 100 *"Make a joyful noise."*

Psalm 103 *"Bless the Lord, O my soul."*

Psalm 116:15 *"Precious in the sight of the Lord is the death of faithful ones."*

Psalm 117 *(two verses) Praise for God's steadfast love and faithfulness.*

Psalm 118:19 *"Open to me the gates of righteousness."*

Psalm 119:28 *"My heart melts away for sorrow; strengthen me according to your word."*

Psalm 121 *"I lift up my eyes to the hills."*

Psalm 124:8 *"Our help is in the name of the Lord, who made heaven and earth."*

Psalm 130 *"Out of the depths I cry to you, O Lord."*

Psalm 139 *"O Lord, you have searched me and known me."*

Psalm 145:17–19 *The Lord is just, near, fulfills desire, hears cry, saves.*

Psalm 146 *God helps, sets prisoners free, opens eyes, lifts up, watches over, upholds.*

Psalm 150 *"Let everything that breathes praise the Lord."*

Proverbs 1:24–33 *Waywardness kills, but those who listen to God are secure.*

Proverbs 3:5, 6, 24 *"Trust in the Lord with all your heart."*

Proverbs 9:10a *"The fear of the Lord is the beginning of wisdom."*

Proverbs 11:16 *"A gracious woman gets honor."*

Proverbs 17:27 *"One who spares words is knowledgeable."*

Proverbs 18:24 *"A true friend sticks closer than one's nearest kin."*

Proverbs 22:1–4 *"A good name is to be chosen rather than great riches."*

Proverbs 27:1 *"Do not boast about tomorrow, for you do not know what a day may bring."*

Proverbs 31 *Attributes of virtuous women.*

Ecclesiastes 3:1–13 *"For everything there is a season ... "*

Ecclesiastes 7:1–6, 20 *Death and mourning are better than birth and laughter.*

Ecclesiastes 12:1–7 *"Remember your Creator in the days of your youth ... "*

Isaiah 1:18b *"Though your sins are like scarlet, they shall be like snow."*

Isaiah 25:6–10 *The Lord will make a feast and wipe away the tears from all faces.*

Isaiah 26:4 *"Trust in the Lord forever, for in the Lord God you have an everlasting rock."*

Isaiah 30:15 *"In returning and rest, you shall be saved; in quietness and in trust shall be your strength."*

Isaiah 32:18 *People abide in peaceful habitations, secure dwellings, quiet resting places.*

Isaiah 33:15·17 *The upright live on the heights with food and water supplied.*

Isaiah 40:8 *The grass withers, but the word of God endures.*

Isaiah 40:11 *"He will feed his flock like a shepherd."*

Isaiah 40:31 *Those who wait for the Lord renew their strength and rise on eagles' wings.*

Isaiah 41:10, 13 *"Do not fear, for I am with you"—to strengthen, uphold, help.*

Isaiah 43:1–3 *"When you pass through the waters, I will be with you" (v. 2a).*

Isaiah 53 *The Suffering Servant—"All we like sheep have gone astray."*

Isaiah 55:1–3, 6–13 *"Come to the waters" (v. 1b), "seek the Lord while he may be found" (v. 6a).*

Isaiah 57:1–2 *The righteous are taken from calamity and enter into peace.*

Isaiah 61:1–3 *"The Spirit of the Lord God is upon me "(v. 1a)— to bring good news and liberty.*

Isaiah 63:8–9 *God's presence and love saved, redeemed, lifted and carried them.*

Isaiah 64:4 *God works for those who wait for God.*

Isaiah 66:13 *As a mother comforts her child, God comforts us.*

Jeremiah 18:1–6 *People of God are like clay in a potter's hands.*

Jeremiah 29:11 *God's plans for your welfare; a future with hope.*

Jeremiah 31:3, 25 *"I have loved you with an everlasting love." Satisfy the weary.*

Lamentations 3:21–23, 33 *God's love, mercies are new every morning; great is your faithfulness. God does not willingly afflict or grieve anyone.*

Ezekiel 18:29, 32 *Is God unfair? There is no pleasure in anyone's death; "turn, then, and live."*

Ezekiel 34:15–16, 23–25 *God is the Good Shepherd who gathers the flock.*

Ezekiel 36:25–28 *God cleanses, gives heart of flesh for heart of stone.*

Daniel 12:2–3, 13 *The dead awake; the wise shine like stars.*

Hosea 14:8c *"I am like an evergreen cypress; your faithfulness comes from me."*

Micah 6:8 *What does God require? Do justice, love kindness, walk humbly.*

Nahum 1:7 *"The Lord is good, a stronghold in a day of trouble."*

Habbakuk 2:20 *The Lord is in holy temple; let all earth keep silence.*

Zephaniah 3:17 *God will rejoice over you with gladness, renew you in love.*

Matthew 5:4 *"Blessed are those who mourn."*

Matthew 5:16 *"Let your light shine."*

Matthew 6:9–13 *(Lord's Prayer) or "Our Father."*

Matthew 6:19–34 *Store your treasures in heaven.*

Matthew 7:7–11 *Ask, search, knock.*

Matthew 7:12 *(Golden Rule) "Do to others as you would have them do to you."*

Matthew 7:24–27 *Wise and foolish builders.*

Matthew 8:11 *Many will come from east and west, to eat in the kingdom of heaven.*

Matthew 10:29–31 *God sees the sparrow fall. Hairs of head numbered; do not fear.*

Matthew 11:25–30 *Come to me all you that are weary … and I will give you rest (v. 28).*

Matthew 17:14–21 *Epileptic child healed; the power of faith the size of mustard seed.*

Matthew 18:1–5, 10–14 *Child is greatest in kingdom of heaven; take care of little ones.*

Matthew 19:13 *"Let the little children come to me."*

Matthew 22:23–32 *In resurrection, like angels;*
  greatest commandment is love.
Matthew 25:31–40 *Angels, glory, the sheep and the goats,*
  eternal life or punishment.
Matthew 28:1–9 *Jesus's resurrection.*
Matthew 28:18–20 *(Great Commission) "Go make disciples …*
  I am with you always."
Mark 4:35 *"Let us go across to the other side."*
Mark 4:36–41 *Jesus calms the storm.*
Mark 9:2–7 (Matthew 17:1–8, Luke 9:28–36)
  Jesus is transfigured—with Moses and Elijah.
Mark 10:13–16 *Let the children come; receive kingdom of God*
  as a child to enter.
Mark 12:28–31 *(Great Commandment) Love God, and love*
  your neighbor.
Luke 2:25–38 *Devout Simeon and prophet Anna see baby Jesus;*
  Simeon is ready to depart in peace.
Luke 4:18 *"The Spirit of the Lord is upon me."*
Luke 6:38 *"Give and it will be given unto you."*
Luke 9:28-36 *Transfiguration.*
Luke 12:22–31 *"Do not worry about your life."*
Luke 12:32 *"Do not be afraid."*
Luke 15:3–7 *The joy of the shepherd who leaves the ninety-nine*
  sheep to find one lost sheep.
Luke 16:19–31 *The rich man in Hades and poor man with*
  angels and Abraham.
Luke 18:13, 16 *Pharisee and tax collector: "God, be merciful*
  to me, a sinner."
Luke 23:39–43 *Jesus to dying thief: "Today you will*
  be with me in Paradise."
Luke 24:5 *Angel to women at tomb, "Why look for the living*
  among the dead?"
John 1:1–14 *In beginning was the Word; Word became flesh*
  and lived among us.

John 1:12 *As many as received, to them he gave power.*

John 3:3–8 *Jesus and Nicodemus—born again.*

John 3:16–17 *For God so loved the world; not to condemn but to save.*

John 3:11–21, 36 *Whoever believes in Christ may have eternal life.*

John 4:27–38 *Jesus and the woman at the well.*

John 5:24–29 *Whoever believes has eternal life; those in graves come forth.*

John 6:37–40 *The will of God—all who believe have eternal life; raised up on last day.*

John 10:1–16 *I am the Good Shepherd.*

John 10:27–30 *Life abundant.*

John 11 *Death and raising of Lazarus.*

John 11:25–26 *"I am the resurrection and the life."*

John 12:24 *A grain of wheat falls into the earth and dies.*

John 13:31–35 *"I am with you only a little longer" (v. 33). "love one another" (v. 34).*

John 14:1–7 *"Do not let not your hearts be troubled" (v. 1). House with many rooms prepared.*

John 14:15–29 *Jesus leaving, not orphaned, promise of Holy Spirit given.*

John 15:1–5, 9-17 *Vine and branches; "love one another" (v. 12).*

John 16:33 *"In me you may have peace."*

John 17:3, 20–24 *Eternal life is knowing God; Jesus prays that all may be one.*

John 20 *Jesus's resurrection; Mary meets Jesus, grief is turned to joy.*

John 21:1–14 *Jesus cooks breakfast for disciples at Galilee.*

Acts 1:9–11 *Jesus's ascension, promise of return.*

Acts 7:55–60 *Stoning of Stephen—who sees heavens open, commits spirit, forgives.*

Acts 9:36–43 *Peter and the raising of Tabitha/Dorcas.*

Romans 5:1–8 *Justified, we have peace; suffering, endurance, character, hope.*

Romans 6:3–9 *Baptized, buried, and raised with Christ.*

Romans 6:23 *Wages of sin is death, but the gift of God is eternal life.*

Romans 8:1–8, 14–18, 28–39 *Nothing can separate us from the love of God.*

Romans 10:13 *"Everyone who calls on the name of the Lord shall be saved."*

Romans 12:15 *Rejoice with those who rejoice, weep with those who weep.*

Romans 12:16–21 *Live peaceably with all; feed enemies; overcome evil with good.*

Romans 14:7–9 *Whether we live or die, we are the Lord's.*

I Corinthians 2:1–9 *Wisdom from God's Spirit; glory beyond human understanding.*

I Corinthians 13 *Eulogy of love, the preeminent virtue.*

I Corinthians 15 *Christ's resurrection; significance and nature of Christ's resurrection and victory over death.*

II Corinthians 1:2–7 *Sharing in suffering and consolation.*

II Corinthians 3:18 *Transformed into (Christ's) image from one degree of glory to another.*

II Corinthians 4:7–10 *Treasure in clay jars—afflicted but not crushed.*

II Corinthians 4:16, 5:8 *Outer/inner nature, tabernacle/temple, natural/spiritual body.*

II Corinthians 5:7 *Walking by faith, not by sight.*

II Corinthians 5:16–21 *In Christ, a new creation, ministry of reconciliation.*

II Corinthians 8:9 *Christ who was rich became poor so we might be rich.*

Galatians 2:20 *No longer I who live, but Christ who lives in me.*

Galatians 5:22–26 *The fruit of the Spirit—for living the Spirit-led life.*

Galatians 6:9–10 *"You reap whatever you sow."*

Ephesians 1:3–14 *Blessed, forgiven, adopted, sealed.*

Ephesians 2:3–4, 4–9 *God's great love given while we were yet sinners.*

Ephesians 3:14–21 *Rooted and grounded in love—Christ dwelling in hearts.*

Ephesians 4:11–16 *Spiritual gifts to equip saints, build up body of Christ.*

Ephesians 5:1–2, 15–17 *Be imitators of God; live in love; be wise, not foolish.*

Ephesians 6:7–8 *Serve with enthusiasm as to God, not people.*

Philippians 1:21 *Living is Christ; dying is gain.*

Philippians 2:1–2 *Encouragement, consolation, and sharing make Christian joy complete.*

Philippians 3:20–21 *Our citizenship in heaven; human bodies transformed to glorious bodies.*

Philippians 4:5–9 *Rejoicing in God always leads to peace, abundant living.*

Philippians 4:11 *"I have learned to be content."*

Philippians 4:13 *"I can do all things through Christ which strengtheneth me." (KJV)*

Colossians 1:3–4 *Praying thanks for faith, love and hope of all the saints.*

Colossians 3:1–4 *Set minds on things above,*

I Thessalonians 4:13–18 *Not ignorant, but grieving with resurrection hope—meet Christ in air.*

I Thessalonians 5:23 *The God of peace sanctifies and keeps.*

II Thessalonians 2:16–17 *God comforts and strengthens.*

I Timothy 6:7 *We brought nothing into the world and take nothing out.*

II Timothy 1:7–10 *God gives spirit of power, love, self-discipline, grace in suffering.*

II Timothy 4:6–8 *Fought the good fight, finished race, kept faith—receive crown.*

Titus 2:11–18 *Grace of God brings salvation, training, growth in faith and works.*

Titus 3:4–7 *God's love saves, renews, blesses, and leads to hope of eternal life.*

Hebrews 3:12–15 *Partners with Christ, holding firm to the end.*

Hebrews 4:14–16 *Christ sympathizes with our weaknesses and offers mercy and grace in our time of need.*

Hebrews 9:27–28 *Christ will appear a second time to save those who eagerly await.*

Hebrews 11 *Definition and examples of faith, "the faith hall of fame."*

Hebrews 12:1–3, 14 *Surrounded by cloud of witnesses, believers persevere and pursue peace.*

Hebrews 13:1–6 *Let mutual love and hospitality continue; some may entertain angels unawares.*

James 1:2–5 *Consider it joy when tested; testing brings endurance, maturity, wisdom.*

James 3:13–18 *Earthly wisdom vs. true wisdom that comes from God.*

James 4:13–16 *Live with knowledge that human life is a mist; live by God's mercy.*

I Peter 1:3–12 *Rejoicing in salvation, Christ's resurrection, genuine faith.*

I Peter 3:22 *Christ at God's right hand with angels and powers as subjects.*

I Peter 5:7 *Cast all your anxiety on God, who cares for you.*

I John 2:25 *God has promised eternal life.*

I John 3:1–3, 16–18 *God loves us as children; love means laying down our lives for one another.*

I John 5:1–4 *Love means keeping commandments; faith is the victory.*

II John 1–6 *The "elect lady" leads children to walk in truth and love.*

Revelation 1:12–18 *Christ among seven golden lampstands;
    alive forever and ever.*
Revelation 2:10, 13 *Do not fear suffering; be faithful; hold fast.*
Revelation 3:20 *I stand at the door and knock; if you hear
    and open, I will come in.*
Revelation 4:1–6 *Vision of heaven and God's glory.*
Revelation 7:9–17 *Great multitude standing before the Lamb/
    Shepherd who wipes away every tear from their eyes.*
Revelation 14:13 *"Blessed are the dead who from now on
    die in the Lord."*
Revelation 19:6–9 *Multitude's praise in heaven for marriage
    of Lamb and bride.*
Revelation 21:1–7 *Vision of the holy city coming down
    from heaven; renewed creation.*
Revelation 22:1–5, 13 *The river and the tree of life in heaven;
    no night there.*
Wisdom 3:1–9 *Souls of the just are in the hand of God.*
Wisdom 5:15–17 *The just live forever; their reward is with God.*
Ecclesiasticus 44 *Praise for the wise, rich in virtue,
    studying beauty, living at peace.*

Beatitudes of Revelation:
1:3 *"Blessed is the one who reads aloud the words of the prophecy,
    and blessed are those who hear and who keep what is
    written in it."*
14:13 *"Blessed are the dead who from now on die in the Lord."*
16:15 *"Blessed is the one who stays awake and is clothed,
    not going about naked and exposed to shame."*
19:9 *"Blessed are those who are invited to the marriage
    supper of the Lamb."*
22:7 *"Blessed is the one who keeps the words of the prophecy
    of this book."*
22:14 *"Blessed are those who wash their robes, so that they
    will have the right to the tree of life and may enter the city
    by the gates."*

Appendix H 2

Biblical Passages of Death and Resurrection

Following are some biblical references to death rituals including embalming, burial and cremation, mourning, weeping, reconciliation, preparing for death, hospice care, deathbed blessings and instructions, funeral processions, martyrdom, and resurrection experiences.

Genesis 23 *Death of Sarah. Abraham buys a field and establishes a family burial plot in Hebron. The family mourns for Sarah and weeps over her, implying a visitation or wake.*

Genesis 25:5–10 *Death of Abraham. He is buried with Sarah by sons Ishmael and Isaac.*

Genesis 25:12–18 *Death of Ishmael, Abraham's and Hagar's son, who was "gathered to his people." The names of Ishmael's sons, the twelve tribal leaders, are listed.*

Genesis 35:8 *Death of Deborah, Rebekah's nurse (24:59), now a member of Jacob's household. Deborah is buried under an oak below Bethel, the "oak of weeping."*

Genesis 35:16 20 *Death of Rachel, Jacob's wife, near Bethlehem. Jacob sets up a pillar to mark her grave.*

Genesis 35:27 29 *Death of Isaac. Sons Esau and Jacob, now reconciled, bury him together.*

Genesis 47–49 *Jacob prepares for his death, blesses his family, gives instructions for his body to be buried with his ancestors in Hebron, and acknowledges God as the One who has shepherded him all his life long (48:15).*

Genesis 50:1 *Joseph threw himself upon his father, wept over him, and kissed him.*

Genesis 50:2–3 *Jacob is embalmed in a forty-day process.
Egyptians mourned 70 days.*

Genesis 50:4–14 *Jacob's funeral procession from Egypt to Hebron
included a 7-day time of mourning at Atad. His sons fulfilled
his burial instructions.*

Genesis 50:15–21 *Reconciliation between Joseph and his brothers.*

Genesis 50:24–25 *Joseph, near death, asks that his bones be taken
to the promised land.*

Genesis 50:26 *Death of Joseph. He is embalmed, and his body
placed in a coffin in Egypt. Centuries later, Moses honors
Joseph's request (Exodus 13:19), and under the leadership
of Moses' successor Joshua, Joseph's bones were buried in
Shechem in a tract of land Jacob bought from Hamor
(Joshua 24:32). Thousands of years later Joseph's faith is
commended in the "faith hall of fame": "By faith Joseph,
when his end was near, spoke about the exodus of the Israelites
from Egypt and gave instructions about his bones"
(Hebrews 11:22, NIV).*

Deuteronomy 34:5–7 *Death of Moses who is buried by God in
an unknown grave in Moab. "The Israelites grieved for Moses
in the plains of Moab thirty days, until the time of weeping and
mourning was over" (34:8 NIV).*

Numbers 20:22–29 *Death of Aaron, Moses' brother, the first
high priest of Israel, whose garments were transferred to his
son Eleazar. The nation mourned thirty days.*

I Samuel 31 *Death of Saul, Israel's first king, who died with
his sons in battle. The bodies were dishonored, fastened to
the wall of Beth Shan. Men of Jabesh Gilead came by night,
took them down, and burned them. Although cremation
was not a custom, it was apparently done to prevent further
dishonor to the bodies. Bones were buried under the tamarisk
tree at Jabesh; the nation fasted seven days. Later, David
had the bones buried in the family burial grounds of Zela
in Benjamin (II Samuel 21:12–14).*

II Samuel 1:11–12 *David and company mourned, wept, and fasted until evening over the deaths of Saul and Jonathan. They composed a lament (1:17–27).*

II Samuel 3:31–37 *David tore clothing, put on sackcloth, walked in mourning behind the bier of slain General Abner, wept aloud at Abner's tomb, composed a lament, and fasted.*

I Kings 1:1,2:10 *A new idea in hospice care—King David spent his last days unable to keep warm, so his servants got a beautiful girl named Abishag to curl up next to him (I Kings 1:1–4). After giving final instructions to Solomon, David "rested with his fathers and was buried in the City of David" (I Kings 2:10 NIV).*

II Kings 1:17, 3:1, 9:26 *Most of the kings were buried "with their fathers" or "in the City of David." Some, however, were considered too wicked to be buried with honor. Joram's body was thrown in Naboth's vineyard.*

II Chronicles 16:12–14 *Death and royal burial of King Asa, using spices and various blended perfumes. A huge fire is held in his honor.*

I Kings 8:16–24, II Chronicles 21:1–20 *Southern king Jehoram was considered beyond redemption—he had a "horrible bowel disease" as judgment for idolatry and murder. No one mourned his death, and he was not buried with the kings.*

I Kings 11:2-21, II Chronicles 22:10, 23:21 *Athaliah, daughter of Ahab and Jezebel (Northern king and queen), usurped the Southern throne after her son Ahaziah's reign. She killed the whole royal family including her grandchildren. She was dragged from the temple to the horse stables and killed there.*

I Kings 12, II Chronicles 24 *King Joash's uncle Jehoiada, the high priest, was buried with the kings, but Joash had his cousin Zechariah, Jehoiadah's son, stoned for prophesying doom because of disobedience; so Joash was buried in the City of David "but not with the kings."*

II Kings 14:21–22, 15:1–7, II Chronicles 26:1–23 *Azariah was a Southern king who was buried near his fathers on land that belonged to the kings, but not in the kings' tombs because he had leprosy.*

II Kings 16:1–20, II Chronicles 28 *Ahaz was considered evil, so he was buried in Jerusalem but "not with the kings."*

II Kings 20:1–4, II Chronicles 32:24–26, Isaiah 38:1–8 *Hezekiah was given an extra fifteen years after Isaiah told him to prepare to die. The sign of this healing grace was that the sundial went back ten steps.*

II Kings 21:1–18, II Chronicles 33:1–20 *Hezekiah's son Manesseh shed innocent blood but repented and was restored. So he was buried in the palace garden.*

II Kings 22:1, 23:30, II Chronicles 34:1, 36:1 *Josiah began a great reformation movement, and upon his death he was buried with his fathers and the prophet Jeremiah composed laments.*

II Kings 24:8–17, 25:27–30, II Chronicles 36:8–10 *Jehoahaz did evil and was dethroned by the king of Egypt and died in chains in Egypt. Jehoiachin surrendered to King Nebuchadnezzar of Babylon and was taken into exile. Under the succeeding king he was treated kindly, given an allowance, and fed at the king's table until his death.*

II Kings 24:17, 25:26, II Chronicles 36:10–23 *The last Southern king, Zedekiah, was also put in shackles and led to Babylon (2 Kings 24:17, 25:26, 2 Chronicles 36:10–23).*

I Kings 17:17–24 *Prophet Elijah raises a widow's son at Zarephath.*

II Kings 2:11–12 *Elijah goes to heaven in a fiery chariot. The whole chapter is a beautiful transfer of power among the "companies of prophets" from Bethel and Jericho.*

II Kings 13:20–21 *Elisha died. When Israelites were burying a man and Moabite raiders came in the spring, they threw the dead person into Elisha's tomb. When the body touched Elisha's bones, the dead man came to life.*

Ezekiel 37:1–14 *Ezekiel's vision of restoration and resurrection*
   in the midst of national exile—the valley of dry bones
Matthew 9:18–19, 23–25, Mark 5:22–24, 38–42,
   Luke 8:41–42, 49–56 *Jesus raises Jairus's daughter.*
Luke 7:11–15 *Jesus raises the widow's son at Nain.*
John 11:1–44 *The death and raising of Lazarus.*
Matthew 17:1–8, Mark 9:1–8, Luke 9:28–36
   The Transfiguration. Jesus's closest disciples are given a glimpse
   of Moses, Elijah and Jesus in glory.
Matthew 26:6–13, Mark 14:1–9, Luke 7:37–38, John 12:1–8
   A woman anoints Jesus with costly perfume beforehand to
   prepare for his burial.
Matthew 27:32–65, Mark 15:21–47, Luke 23:26–56,
   John 19:17–42 *Jesus's death and burial.*
John 19:38–42 *Joseph of Arimathea and Nicodemus bury Jesus,*
   wrapped in linen strips soaked in myrrh and aloes (about
   seventy-five pounds—as in a royal burial per II Chronicles
   16:14—and in accordance with Jewish burial customs).
Luke 23:55, 24:1 *Women prepare spices and ointments to further*
   embalm Jesus's body.
Matthew 28:1–15, Mark 16:1–14, Luke 24:1–12,
   John 20:1–30 *As women come to anoint Jesus's body with*
   spices very early in the morning on the first day of the week,
   they become the first witnesses of his resurrection.
Acts 6:8–60 *The seizure, speech, and stoning of Stephen,*
   a disciple who saw heaven open and Jesus in glory.
Acts 9:36–42 *The disciple Dorcas dies, her body is washed*
   and placed in an upstairs room, and she is raised after the
   prayers of the disciple Peter.

Appendix I

AFTERCARE: GRIEF SUPPORT RESOURCES

Local Resources:
Resources such as pamphlets, books, audio tapes, videos, and information regarding support groups and grief counselors may be found at:

Funeral homes	Hospice	Hospitals
Churches	Schools	Senior centers
Libraries	Friends	Relatives

Booklets:
CareNotes by Abbey Press (1–800–325–2511; www.carenotes. com) are available in many hospitals, churches, funeral homes, hospice, etc. These brief booklets offer much wisdom. Written by people who've "been there," they offer additional reading resources, and are available in a variety of titles such as:

What Everyone Should Know about the First Year of Grief
When Death Comes Unexpectedly to Someone You Love
12 Reflections for the First 12 Weeks of Grief
A Serenity Prayer for Grievers
Being Angry With God at a Time of Suffering or Loss
Dealing With All the "Stuff" after a Loved One Dies
Finding Your Way After the Death of a Spouse
Five Ways to Get through the First Year of Loss
Getting through the Holidays When You've Lost a Loved One
Dealing with the Anger That Comes with Grief
What's Really "Normal" When You're Grieving?
Why Did My Loved One Have to Die Now?
Overcoming Loneliness after Loss

The Ten Biggest Myths about Grief
Using Good Memories to Help Heal Your Grief
Feeling Overwhelmed by One Loss after Another
Still Grieving after All These Years
Grieving in Your Own Way
What Grieving Does to the Body

CareNotes for Teens:
Anger—When You Feel Like You're Going to Explode
Grieving When You Lose Someone Close

Special Series:
In-Sight Books are written by Doug Manning, a clergyman/funeral director (1-800-658-9262; www.insightbooks.com).
Don't Take My Grief Away from Me
When Love Gets Tough: The Nursing Home Decision
Please Hear of My Lost Love
Lean on Me Gently: Helping the Grieving Child

In-Sight Booklets:
Establishing Significance
Understanding Grief
The Gift of Understanding
Reconstructing Our Lives

I Know Someone Who Died, a coloring book by Connie Manning (wife of Doug) to help children work through grief.

Daily Devotional:
Healing After Loss, Daily Meditations for Working through Grief. Martha Whitmore Hickman. Perennial: 1994.

General Materials:
How to Survive the Loss of a Love. Melba Colgrove, Ph.D., Harold Bloomfield, M.D., and Peter McWilliams. Mary Books: c. 1976, 1991.

The Screaming Room. Barbara Peabody. Avon Books,
New York: 1986—A mother's journal of her son's
struggle with AIDS.

Getting through the Night. Eugenia Price. Ballantine Books,
New York: 1982.

Going Solo. Ted Menten. Running Press, Philadelphia–
London: 1995.

After Goodbye. Ted Menten. Running Press, Philadelphia–
London: 1994.

Gentle Closings. Ted Menten. Running Press, Philadelphia–
London: 1991.

The Four Things That Matter Most. Ira Byock, M.D.
FreePress, New York: 2004.

Dying Well: The Prospect for Growth at the End of Life.
Ira Byock, M.D. Riverhead Books, New York: 1997.

Kitchen Table Wisdom: Stories That Heal. Rachel Naomi
Remen. Riverhead Books, New York: 1996.

On Death and Dying. Elisabeth Kubler-Ross, M.D.
The MacMillan Company, New York: 1969.

Good Grief. Granger E. Westberg. Fortress Press, Philadelphia:
1961.

Books for Children:

Water Bugs and Dragonflies. Doris Stickney. The Pilgrim Press,
Cleveland: 2004.

*A Candle for Grandpa, A Guide to the Jewish Funeral for
Children and Parents.* David Techner and
Judith Hirt-Manheimer. UACH Press, New York: 1993.

Charlotte's Web. E.B. White. HarperCollins Publishers,
New York: 1974.

What's Happening to Grandpa? Maria Shriver. Little,
Brown and Company and Warner Books,
Boston, New York: 2004.

The Redheaded Woman, A Star and Elephant Book.
Helen Eustis. Green Tiger Press, La Jolla, CA: 1950.

When Violet Died. Fred Rogers. G. P. Putnam's Sons,
    New York: 1988.
Lifetimes: The beautiful way to explain death to children ...
    Bryan Mellonie and Robert Ingpen. Bantam Books,
    New York: 1983—uses examples from nature.
The Next Place. Warren Hanson. Waldman House Press, Inc.,
    Minneapolis: 1997.
The Fall of Freddie the Leaf. Leo Buscaglia, Ph.D.
    Holt, Rinehart and Winston, Texas: 1982.
The Tenth Good Thing about Barney. Judith Viorst.
    Aladdin Paperbacks, New York: 1971
What's Heaven? Maria Shriver. St. Martin's Press,
    New York: 1999.
Cat Heaven. Cynthia Rylant. The Blue Sky Press,
    New York: 1997.
I Know Someone Who Died. Connie Manning.
    A coloring book available from In-Sight Books
    (see previous page).

Video:
Tear Soup, A Recipe For Healing After Loss. Pat Schwiebert and
    Chuck Deklyen. GriefWatch, Portland, Oregon: 2003.
    (www.griefwatch.com.)

Especially for Dealing with the Death of Children:
Roses In December. Marilyn Willett Heavilin. Harvest House
    Publishers, Eugene, Oregon: 1987.
*When Winter Follows Spring, Surviving The Death of an
    Adult Child.* Dorothy Ferguson. Centering Corporation,
    Omaha, Nebraska: 2002.
Psalms of Lament. Ann Weems. Westminster John Knox Press,
    Louisville, Kentucky: 1995.

End Notes

Chapter 1

1. Gassman, McDill McCown. *Daddy Was an Undertaker.*
   New York: Vantage Press, 1952.

Chapter 2

1. Kubler-Ross, Elisabeth, M.D. *On Death and Dying.* New
   York: The MacMillan Co., 1969.
2. Schaef, Anne Wilson. *Native Wisdom for White Minds.*
   New York: One World Ballantine Books, 1995.
3. Colgrove, Melba, Ph.D., Harold Bloomfield, M.D.,
   and Peter McWilliams. *How to Survive the Loss
   of a Love.* Allen Park, MI: Mary Books, 1976, 1991.
4. *CareNotes.* St. Meinrad, IN: Abbey Press, Pamphlets.

Chapter 4

1. McRae, Oliver. "Deathcare: Past, Present … and Future."
   The Director. July 2004: 94–95.
2. Lynch, Thomas. "Grave Affairs: HBO's 'Six Feet Under.'"
   The Christian Century, November 2, 2004, p. 18.
3. Albom, Mitch. *The Five People You Meet in Heaven.*
   New York: Hyperion, 2003.
4. Gladstone, William Ewart (1809–1898).

Chapter 5

1. Trible, Phyllis. *God and the Rhetoric of Sexuality.*
   Philadelphia: Fortress Press, 1978.
2. Douglas-Klotz, Neil. *Prayers of the Cosmos.* San Francisco:
   HarperCollins Publishers, 1990.
3. Remen, Rachel Naomi. *Kitchen Table Wisdom, Stories
   That Heal.* New York: Riverhead Books, 1996.

Chapter 6

1. von Franz, Marie-Louise. *Number and Time: Reflections Leading toward Unification of Depth Psychology and Physics.* Andrea Dykes, trans. Evanston, IL: Northwestern Univ. Press, 1974.
2. Brueggeman, Walter. Foreword. *Psalms of Lament.* By Ann Weems. Louisville, KY: Westminster John Knox Press, 1995.

Chapter 7

1. McRae, Oliver. "Deathcare: Past, Present ... and Future." *The Director.* July 2004: 94–95. Updated figures for 2005 provided by publisher.

Chapter 10

1. Hopper, Edward. "Jesus, Saviour, Pilot Me," *Inspiring Hymns.* Compiled by Alfred B. Smith. Grand Rapids, MI: Singspiration, 1951. #64.
2. Buttrick, David. Drucilla Moore Buffington Professor of Homiletics and Liturgics, Emeritus, Vanderbilt Univ., The Divinity School, personal correspondence. 22 January 2004.

Chapter 11

1. Kubler-Ross, Elisabeth, M.D. *On Death and Dying.* New York: The MacMillan Co. 1969.
2. Westberg, Granger E. *Good Grief: A Constructive Approach to Death and Dying.* Philadelphia: Augsburg Fortress Publishers, 1961.
3. Colgrove, Melba, Ph.D., Harold Bloomfield, M.D., and Peter McWilliams. *How To Survive The Loss Of A Love.* Allen Park, MI: Mary Books, 1976, 1991.
4. *CareNotes.* St. Meinrad, IN: Abbey Press, Pamphlets.

5. Cowper, William. (c. 1772) "God Moves in a
   Mysterious Way," *Psalter Hymnal*. Grand Rapids, MI:
   The Publication Committee of the Christian
   Reformed Church, c. 1934.
6. Johns, Rob (c. 1983). "In Suffering Love," *Songs For
   A Gospel People*. Winfield, BC, Canada:
   Wood Lake Books Inc., 1991.
7. Kovanis, Georgea. "The Bride Was Beautiful."
   Detroit Free Press. 30 January 2005.

Bibliography

Albom, Mitch. *The Five People You Meet in Heaven.*
New York: Hyperion, 2003.

Brueggeman, Walter. Foreword. *Psalms of Lament.*
By Ann Weems. Louisville, KY: Westminster John
Knox Press, 1995.

Buttrick, David. Drucilla Moore Buffington
Professor of Homiletics and Liturgics, Emeritus,
Vanderbilt Univ., The Divinity School.
Personal correspondence. 22 January 2004.

CareNotes. St. Meinrad, IN: Abbey Press.

Colgrove, Melba, Ph.D., Bloomfield, Harold, M.D.,
and McWilliams, Peter. *How to Survive the Loss of
a Love,* Allen Park, MI: Mary Books, 1976, 1991.

Cowper, William. (c. 1772) "God Moves in a
Mysterious Way." *Psalter Hymnal.* Grand Rapids, MI:
The Publication Committee of the Christian
Reformed Church, 1934.

Douglas-Klotz, Neil. *Prayers of the Cosmos.* San Francisco:
HarperCollins, Publishers, 1990.

Gassman, McDill McCown. *Daddy Was an Undertaker.*
New York: Vantage Press, 1952.

Hagberg, Janet O. *Real Power, Stages of Personal Power in Organizations*. Salem, WI: Sheffield Publishing Company, 1994, 1984.

Hopper, Edward. "Jesus, Saviour, Pilot Me." *Inspiring Hymns*. Grand Rapids, MI: Compiled by Alfred B. Smith. Singspiration, 1951.

Johns, Rob. (c. 1983) "In Suffering Love." *Songs for a Gospel People*. Winfield, BC, Canada: Wood Lake Books Inc., 1991.

Kovanis, Georgea. "The Bride Was Beautiful." *Detroit Free Press*. 30 January 2005: 1G–3G.

Kubler-Ross, Elisabeth, M.D. *On Death and Dying*. New York: The MacMillan Company, 1969.

Lynch, Thomas. "Grave Affairs." *The Christian Century*. 2 November 2004.

McRae, Oliver. "Deathcare: Past, Present … and Future." *The Director*. July 2004.

Middleton, John. *Encyclopedia Americana*. Vol. 8, p. 568. Danbury, CT: Scholastic Library Publishing, Inc., 2004.

Remen, Rachel Naomi. *Kitchen Table Wisdom: Stories That Heal*. New York, New York: Riverhead Books, 1996.

Schaef, Anne Wilson. *Native Wisdom for White Minds*. New York: One World Book Ballantine Books, 1995.

Sheehy, Gail. *Passages: Predictable Crises of Adult Life*.
New York: E.P. Dutton & Co. Inc., 1974, 1976.

Trible, Phyllis. *God and the Rhetoric of Sexuality*. Philadelphia:
Augsburg Fortress Publishers, 1978.

Viorst, Judith. *Necessary Losses: The Loves, Illusions,
Dependencies, and Impossible Expectations That All of Us
Have to Give Up in Order to Grow*. Fireside, NY:
c. 1986, first Fireside Edition, 1998.

von Franz, Marie-Louise. *Number and Time: Reflections
Leading Toward a Unification of Depth Psychology
and Physics*. Andrea Dykes, trans.
Northwestern Univ. Press, Evanston, IL: 1974.

Westberg, Granger E. *Good Grief: A Constructive Approach
to Death and Dying*. Philadelphia: Fortress Press, 1961.

World Book Encyclopedia. 2004 Edition, Volume 7, p. 558.

ABOUT THE AUTHOR

Celia M. Hastings holds a master's degree in religious education from Western Theological Seminary in Holland, Michigan. She is the author of *The Wisdom Series, a Bible Survey Curriculum for Adults, a Worship Approach to Education in 52 Sessions*. She lives and works with her funeral director husband in a small northern Michigan funeral home where, besides writing, she plays the organ and officiates at funerals.